The Complete
STAFFORDSHIRE
BULL TERRIER

DANNY GILMOUR

RINGPRESS

To my wife, Patsy, and my daughter
Danielle – the two best girls in the world.

RINGPRESS

Published by Ringpress Books Ltd,
PO Box 8, Lydney, Gloucestershire GL15 6YD

Discounts available for bulk orders
Contact the Special Sales Manager at
the above address. Telephone 01594 563800

First Published 1994
© 1994 DANNY GILMOUR

ISBN 0 948955 69 4

Printed and bound in Singapore
by Kyodo Printing Co

CONTENTS

4

ACKNOWLEDGEMENTS

Thanks to Gareth Westerdale (South Africa), Lotte Berg (Denmark), Hilary Harmar (England), George Scherzer (Germany), Heather Maxwell (Holland), and to all the Stafford people all over the world who have sent information and pictures – I am only sorry that we could not use all the contributions. Special thanks to Annette Skelly who so patiently put together all my notes and scribbles, along with all the chopping and changing – it must have driven her near insane! And last but not least, to Frank Dickson, who lit the flame that still burns brightly to this day.

DANNY GILMOUR

FOREWORD

Much has been written about the Staffordshire Bull Terrier and the history of the breed. Indeed, with many excellent reference works at hand for both the experienced owner and the newcomer, a new book, aimed at providing a refreshingly new approach to authoritative works on the breed, is regarded with great interest. Who better than Danny Gilmour to come up with a gem of a book with a difference?

Danny needs little introduction – international show judge of repute, owner of the world-famous Dumbriton affix, breeder of first-class, unmistakably typical stock, formidable opponent in the show ring, and always a controversial character – he has put down on paper his wealth of experience in the breed for the benefit of all who love Staffordshire Bull Terriers.

For this book, much research has gone into the history of the breed, which provides a fascinating insight to the origins of the modern-day Stafford. For both experienced and novice alike, the chapters on every conceivable aspect of Stafford welfare and ownership – from selection of puppies to rearing, breeding, whelping and showing – are a must.

Written sensitively, and always with the welfare of the Stafford in mind, Danny, whenever necessary, has carefully put himself in the position of the newcomer questing for knowledge, giving guidance and help to avoid the pitfalls and dangers arising from bad advice.

This book is, without doubt, unique, and it fully deserves its place among the authoritative works on the Staffordshire Bull Terrier.

JIM BEAUFOY.

INTRODUCTION

To be asked to write a book about Staffordshire Bull Terriers is both flattering and exciting. Flattering because, for a fleeting moment, one can cherish the illusion that what one thinks and writes is of some importance, and exciting because it gives the opportunity to write about all the things which go to make up life with Staffords.There are many things that need to be said on the subject of looking after and caring for this great dog.

Undoubtedly, Staffordshire Bull Terriers are a breed apart. There is something special about them, hard to define, but easily recognisable as one grows to know them. They possess uncanny intelligence, perception, great courage, and — something often lacking in other breeds — a decided sense of humour.

Readers who appreciate these qualities in a dog, and would love to have as a companion a pocket-sized battleship with a king-sized heart, will be content with a Staffordshire Bull Terrier all the days of their lives.

A famous writer said, with such truth, that the love of animals brings suffering indeed, because their life span is so short compared to our own. The same writer thought that animals did not stay so long on earth because they deserve heaven more than we do.

While we are privileged to have them with us, the happiness our dogs bring us cannot be measured in words. It is because I have had this happiness in such measure that I hope this book may enable others to enjoy it too. Those who already know and love the breed may possibly find something within its pages which will add to their pleasure, and to the well-being of their beloved Staffordshire Bull Terriers.

Danny Gilmour, August 1994.

Ch. Skerry Dhu of Dumbriton, owned by Danny Gilmour and Neil Maclean. This top-winning Staffordshire Bull Terrier (pictured at ten months) was unbeaten as a puppy, winning twenty-six firsts, nineteen of them at Championship level.

Chapter One

PROFILE OF THE STAFFORD

EARLY HISTORY

Information from the sporting writers of days gone by tells us of the crossing between Bulldogs and Terriers, the results of which are borne out by the name 'Bull Terrier'. The first person to refer to the dog by this name was a Scotsman called Captain Thomas Brown, who in his *Biographical Sketches & Authentic Anecdotes of Dogs* (1829) devoted a complete chapter to the Bull Terrier in which he described the Duke of Hamilton's breed to a T.

VARIATION IN TYPE

We must bear in mind that people in the Fancy had bred the Bulldog to their own preference, which meant there were some dogs at 25lbs and others at 60lbs. This represented quite a variation, but it was every man to his own liking, be it cockfighting, dogfighting, badger baiting, rat killing, bull baiting and so on. All these Bulldogs had longer legs than present day Bulldogs. If you study the picture of the little girl and the Bulldog of about 60lbs, you can see those long legs, well-tucked-in elbows, level topline, strong hindquarters, and pump-handle tail, although the head is starting to look like the modern Bulldog. I consider it more than likely that this was the type they developed their dog from, the lighter 25lb type being more in line with our present day Staffordshire Bull Terrier.

In the twentieth century the fighting reputation of these dogs and their owners was still very much in evidence. Joe Mallam & Co. still kept this sport to the fore, and in fact I remember Joe telling me at Birmingham Championship Show of some of the battles that took place in the cellar of the old Crossguns pub. Some of these dogs were only about 25lbs, and the peculiar thing about these little battlers was that most of them were undershot. To say I was amazed is an understatement, as I had always been led to believe that the smaller terrier-type dogs were the ones with perfect mouths. How wrong we were to assume this to be correct! It has become evident that these smaller dogs were, in fact, the small Bulldog that we know existed in the early nineteenth century.

Joe Dunn, writing as Breed correspondent for the magazine *Our Dogs* in 1947, said that it was very rare to see good examples of the 25lb dog. Mr Amos Smith always said that he never kept a dog of more than 32lbs. and he was President of the Staffordshire Bull Terrier Club. In fact, he spoke at great length about 22lb bitches and 24lb dogs that he knew of in 1947. Mr Baldrey of Accrington asked Mr Dunn in his notes, also in 1947, about the demise of the 24lb dog. Mr Dunn explained that, in his opinion, Mr Jack Kinsey was the best breeder of this type of dog, and goes on to say that Mr Kinsey's best dog was called Leston Boy, who was pied, and of outstanding quality, except for his faulty mouth. He was regarded as one of the best dogs of his time. Mr

Kinsey came from the Bilston area, and his dogs were renowned for their gameness.

Prior to Kennel Club recognition in 1935, three types were in evidence in the Black Country. The Cradley type were short-backed, stocky dogs of cobby type. The Warlaston type, the lightweights so often referred to, were low to ground with a terrier-like contour, and the Walsall type were terrier-type again, but up on the leg.

THE WHITE STRAIN
Between 1850 and 1860, Mr James Hinks of Birmingham, who always liked a game dog, produced a white strain which he had registered at the Kennel Club as The Bull Terrier. Mr Hinks had crossed the old type dog with English White Terriers. This new breed retained all the gameness of the old type, but was vastly different in the head shape, and looks were the main commodity paying dividends in the show ring. The original breed, which was still unspoilt by crossing with dogs not bred for gameness, was now barred from the official title of Bull Terrier. It gradually became known as the Brindle Bull in the London area and the Staffordshire Bull Terrier in the Midlands, and the latter name was eventually accepted by most people in the Fancy — the colliers, chainmakers and ironworkers of Staffordshire. The main fraternity, still strongly attached to dog-fighting and the Sport, had become localised in the Midlands.

THE FIGHTING FRATERNITY
Half a century went by with no reduction in the popularity of dog-fighting, despite spasmodic brushes with the police. Nothing had been done to standardise any type, for courage and physical fitness were still the only things that mattered. Any dog which proved unusually successful in the pit was certain to be used as a sire, irrespective of his looks, and there was still a wide variation of types which, as we said earlier, had become curiously localised, i.e. the Cradley, the Warlaston and the Walsall types. The Walsall men said that theirs were the only "real" Staffords, but in all honesty, who could say that one type is right and the other is wrong, and who could argue that this dog is a "real" Stafford and that one is not? A few years ago nobody minded very much, so long as each was willing to give a good account of itself in the pit — but all that has changed now.

THE SHOW STAFFORD
In the early thirties, a group of owners thought it might be a good idea to arrange dog-shows as an alternative attraction to dog-fights. Accordingly, a schedule was drawn up to determine a scale of points for judging and the Kennel Club obliged by recognising the breed as the Staffordshire Bull Terrier. It was natural that the men who drew up the scale of points should model the ideal from their own particular strains, which happened to be Bulldoggy in type, in favour of the Cradley district.

The results have been very far-reaching. Due to the publicity acquired from organised dog shows, the popularity of Staffords has soared and their market value has been inflated in the same ratio. This has attracted a new type of owner, interested more in the Show type than in the gameness of the breed. He is loud in his assertion that the Show type is right, and that the Show enthusiast will standardise the breed and eradicate everything which does not conform to the standard.

I think there are still people who feel very sorry about all this, for they consider it a great pity to try to breed out all the types which do not conform to such an arbitrary standard. To them, fighting was the original purpose of the breed, yet they point out that all dogs, except those who waddle round the show ring without any display of fire, are penalised.

I have heard long arguments about which type was best for the pit. Some liked a reachy dog, like

Ch. Mistress McGrath of Boldmore: The Staffordshire Bull Terrier, bred originally as a fighting dog, is highly-prized for its bold and fearless character.

the old Walsall strain, because he could "fight down" on his adversaries. Some preferred the stocky Cradley type because they were hard to knock off their feet, and yet others championed the little terrier-like dog which was so nippy and could do so much damage by shaking. In the pit, one would triumph one day and another the next. Despite the fact that failures were not given the opportunity to perpetuate their like, there were so many good dogs of each type that there could have been nothing to choose between them for prowess.

The fighting fraternity were quite scathing in their attacks on people out to make money by selling their pedigree dogs at inflated prices, and inducing owners not only to standardise to an arbitrary type, but to exaggerate the point of that type, so that it becomes more powerful, thicker, lower to the ground and bigger in skull than was any dog that fought in the pit.

VARIATION IN TEMPERAMENT

This extraordinary variation in type was by no means confined to physical appearance — all good Staffords are game — but some are essentially boisterous and rough, while others are equally docile and gentle, both characteristics being passed on through strains as definitely as physical appearance. Two very famous dogs, who exhibited these tendencies to a marked degree, were UK Ch. Gentleman Jim and the Great Bomber. Jim was all that his name implied and, generally speaking, his offspring are tractable, intelligent and easily-trained. Bomber, on the other hand, just could not keep still, overflowed with boisterous friendliness, and was extremely headstrong. His type needs an exceptionally firm hand to control, whereas it is very easy to hurt the gentle type's feelings and deeply offend them with a few hard words.

THE NEED FOR FIRM HANDLING

No dogs are physically tougher than Staffords, for they seem almost impervious to pain. It has been known for a Stafford who was broken to ferrets to go into the ferret pen to see what it could

Ch. Indiana Acid Queen, bred by Mr and Mrs Curd, owned by Hanaway and Curd. The Stafford was accepted as a show dog in the thirties, and since then the breed has soared in popularity.

scrounge. One of the ferrets pinned it through the lip and hung on, which must have been pretty painful, yet the bitch did not get annoyed or make any fuss, but calmly found her owner so that he could throttle it off.

It is this indifference to pain which makes Staffies such peerless fighting dogs. Almost any dog will fight if he is winning, but it takes an exceptional dog to fight a long, losing battle and then go back for more. A good Stafford will go back as long as he can crawl. Despite this, the breed is not naturally pugnacious and it is unusual for a Stafford to begin his first fight. He is either set on by someone, or attacked and fights back in self-defence. However, once he (or she, for bitches will fight) has tried fighting, there is nothing they would rather do. That is why I advise no one but a real enthusiast to embark upon the ownership of one of these dogs.

The man who wants a dog for a household pet, but expects it to run loose and look after itself, will soon regret his choice. It has been known for Staffords to run loose in the streets and play with other dogs for two or three years, but sooner or later they either get hurt playing or get mixed up in someone else's quarrel, and suddenly they realise what fun they have been missing. From that time forth they need no second invitation and will fight to kill. Neither water nor any of the usual remedies will part them. My wife once experienced a fight between two of our own dogs, one a Champion Stafford and the other a Champion Whippet. They ended up in the canal, and if she had not thought quickly and pulled them out by the scruffs of their necks, they would have drowned. Remember, this was a case of two dogs who had lived and gone out for walks with each other for five years – a perfect case of something else upsetting them, and before you know it, there is a confrontation. Owners who are not enthusiastic are often adverse to getting sufficiently mixed up in the bother to choke their dog off, which is the only effective way of dealing with it.

Anyone willing to take the necessary pains to train and exercise a potential handful of trouble will be amply rewarded by finding it far less onerous than he thought. You will get devotion undreamed of in lesser breeds. You will possess a dog who is a peerless companion for children, though it will be necessary to watch that he doesn't "help" too vigorously if his young master has a quarrel with a playmate. You will have an animal who will be quick to kill that unwanted rat. I even trained my Ch. Torosay Black Fern to be a very fine gundog, who would quarter as well as any Pointer, retrieve from water, and go into bramble or thornbush better than most Spaniels. Having said that, most Staffords don't like water, but if you introduce them gradually and in warm weather if possible, taking things a wee bit at a time, yours will try to please you.

The Stafford is a dog of very exceptional character. Take great pains to develop this and direct it into useful channels, and you will find no breed in the world as good.

Chapter Two

ORIGINS OF THE BREED

The Staffordshire Bull Terrier has a long and fascinating history, and the breed's ancestors can be traced back for thousands of years. In discussing the early type of progenitors, I am talking about dogs that preceded the Bulldog, i.e. the Fighting Mastiff.

DOGS OF WAR

Recent excavations at Catal-Huyuk in Turkey have brought to light a veritable sanctuary of ritual hunting scenes dating from about 6,000 B.C. These show bearded men surrounding and harrying an enormous bull which is being attacked by their dogs.

It is from Assyria that we have inherited the impressive brachycephalic dogs which originated in Tibet, and Sumerian cuneiform inscriptions enable us to trace the frightening mastiff dogs as far back as 3,500 B.C. This is a remarkable fact, and proof that man had indeed domesticated these animals. The same ideogram is used to denote this dog, the servant, the valet and the slave.

In the Berlin Museum, as in the British Museum and the Louvre, we can get a good idea of the descendants of these great, fierce dogs, from the admirable bas-reliefs of Assurbanipal (900 B.C.). Also in the British Museum is the famous Sumerian bowl which has engraved on its sides a wild boar hunt with mastiffs at the boar's throat and hindquarters. This hunt took place in the marshes of Babylon round about 3,000 B.C. When the Assyrian Empire crumbled, the Medes, Persians and all the hunting kings of the Orient paid enormous sums for these magnificent dogs, whose role seems to have been as important as that of the greyhound in the history of the canine race.

Persia was probably one of the first nations to use the mastiff as a dog of war. People worshipped them like gods, in fact, and although it was allowable to destroy lizards, worms and harmful insects, to kill a dog was a crime, and to cherish it a duty. So decreed Ormund the Son of Fire. The ancients did not hesitate to give their great and wise men the name of Chan ("The Dog") as a symbolic appellation of the spirit of gentleness and wisdom.

The great men of Persia – the Kings in particular – used the most ferocious of these mastiffs as dogs of war on every battlefield. Cyrus the Great, in the course of his campaigns, exempted four towns in Babylon from all taxes, charging them with the breeding and training of the most cruel combat Mastiffs for his armies. These dogs were also savagely set upon prisoners and traitors.

The Indo-European semi-pastoral people came from the same region as the Persians, and from the time of the second millennium B.C. they emigrated towards western and southern Europe. As soon as they had the horse, they became fearsome warriors and, accompanied by their ravening mastiffs, they invaded the Fertile Crescent from Babylon to Egypt.

We then move on to the Hyksos (circa 2100-1850 B.C.), a race of people who were in control of Egypt. Their true origin is still obscure, although we know that they introduced bronze and the horse into the Nile valley. But where did they come from and who were they? The Egyptians carefully obliterated every trace of these intelligent and artistic strangers to whom they owed a great deal. The Hyksos changed the face of Egypt, and from them sprang a new Egypt. Did these small, strapping Hyksos, with their chariots, horses and dogs, come from the steppes of Central Asia? Like all Egypt's invaders (Hurrians, Hittites and Semites) they brought a great deal to the kingdom, but they allowed themselves to be assimilated by her. Did they bring the mastiff to Egypt? It is quite likely that they did. In any case, before them there are no Egyptian documents to be found representing this formidable, hefty, and powerful dog, which would have been of no use for hunting water-fowl or antelope.

The Egyptians freed themselves from the Hyksos, but they kept the mastiff. Queen Hatshepsut sent emissaries to the land of Punt to give the ruler some of her finest mastiffs. The Egyptian dog was now invested with a new role. This newcomer, the mastiff, became the soldier's dog, or more exactly, the "devouring dog", who was set on the fleeing enemy. In Cairo Museum there is a Persian miniature which shows the famous Pharaoh Tutankhamen (1352 B.C.) standing upright in his chariot, shooting arrows at routed Nubian soldiers, who are being harried by his Assyrian dogs. These powerful, cream-coloured mastiffs, who wore wide collars armed with wrought-iron spikes, must have terrified the enemy.

EUROPEAN INFLUENCE

Turning our attention to Europe, we come to the Gauls, descended from the Indo-Europeans who had settled in western and southern Europe. The Gauls inherited their ancestors' love of the Dogs of War, and their dogs were no less fearful than the ones of old. In fact, when the Celts and the Cimbri were defeated by the Romans, it took two days of fierce battle against the dogs of the enemy, who alone defended their chariots and baggage.

Xerxes introduced the heavy, powerful dog into Greece, and later Alexander the Great, on his return from India, brought back a very similar type of dog. They were to be his Dogs of War and the ancestors of the dogs of Macedonia and Epirus. The King of Albania sent Alexander the Great a dog so accomplished at fighting that he said: "Bears or boars or any other race of dog is no match for such dogs as these; bestow on this one that I send you at least an elephant or lion." The second day after the dog's arrival, it disembowelled the lion and killed the elephant. Filled with admiration, Alexander was ever after to hold this dog in fraternal affection.

In Rome too, these terrible dogs, ferocious and fierce combatants, were adored, and their image is often found on oil lamps. From the 5th century, Rome sent some of these dogs into the Province of Vindossia (the modern Brugg) in Switzerland, where the complete and perfectly-preserved skeleton of one of them was recently discovered. Later, these dogs accompanied Roman expeditions into Germania, where canine remains have been found in excavations in Wurtemberg. The Romans, being a soldierly race, were able to appreciate the military qualities of the mastiff, and they made him an integral part of their triumphant expeditions. These attacking dogs were clad in heavy iron collars, and carried cutting points and sharp blades fixed on their sides and backs. The Romans, too, called them "devouring dogs", and starved them for two days before they went into combat.

The Phoenicians were a race of people who took their dogs with them on all seafaring journeys and they used the mastiff to repel pirates from boarding their vessels. They also used them as Dogs of War in their battles with some of the tribes they encountered on their voyages up the coast of France and into the Irish Sea. Some of their Dogs of War were left behind with the Irish tribes. Interestingly, the Phoenicians used the Canary Isles as a stopping-off point – in fact, their dogs were so favoured by the locals that the Canaries became known as the Islands of the Dogs.

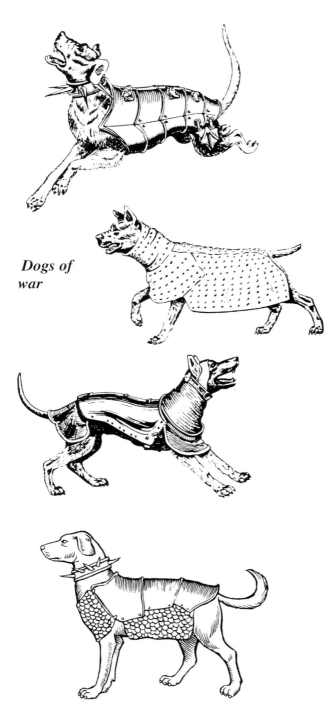

Dogs of war

The Celts who settled in Gaul in the 5th century B.C. were a very artistic race of people, as we know from surviving artefacts. The very fine artwork on the famous Cauldron of Gundestrap in the National Museum, Copenhagen, includes a raised plaque showing some bulls being harassed by aggressive dogs. These dogs are of medium size. This type of dog became very highly prized, and Julius Caesar himself set a high value on them. "The Gauls," wrote Roman commentator Arrian, "take a great pride in the ability of their dogs to perform with cunning and speed and to be able to hold on with strength of jaw that no other canine can compare with."

When Gaul became part of the Roman Empire, the chieftains of Gaul took great pains to send their conquerors the best examples of their Dogs of War. Bituit, king of Arverne, offered his own dogs as gifts to the Consul Domitius in 122 B.C. No one could deny that ancient Gaul had a spirit of generosity and pride in their dog's ability.

THE BULLDOG AND MASTIFF IN BRITAIN

The name bulldog was given, obviously, to dogs that fought bulls! He took his size and general make and shape from the smaller of the two mastiff types of dog in abundance at that time. The mastiff had been in existence since the Celtic days. The warlike tribes in Ireland had used their hunting hounds as guard dogs, as well as a heavier strain which they took into battle with them. When the Irish Celtic tribe known as the Scots captured the west coast of Scotland

The very fine artwork on this famous Celtic piece, known as Cauldron of Gundestrap, includes this scene of a bull being harrassed by dogs.

(then known as Dalriada) they took with them their Dogs of War. Over the years, other tribes soon saw the benefits of having this type of dog. One of these Celtic tribes was the Britons who came from Dumbarton, the ancient capital of Strathclyde (Dumbarton means the Fort of the Britons.)

When the Celtic tribes moved south into England and Wales, they settled in Cornwall with their dogs. In East Anglia the Iceni tribe rampaged with their queen, Boadicea, who terrified the Romans with her ferocious warriors and equally ferocious War Dogs. The Romans called them the "broad-mouthed dogs of Britain"and shipped the animals back to Rome, to fight in the amphitheatres. The dogs acquitted themselves very well in these battles, and their fame soon became widespread. The Romans took their new "fighting machines", described as of gigantic size, a yellowish colour with a black mask, to the countries they conquered in Europe. This new dog was used by the locals on their own dogs to produce new varieties. It is certain that most of Europe's modern big breeds owe their type to the old fighting mastiff of many centuries ago.

In England, the difference in the size of the mastiff has continued through the centuries, the larger one being used for baiting sports. In the time of Henry VIII, the smaller one was known as the band-dogge or butcher's dog, and was the forerunner of our bulldog. The close similarity between the two dogs goes without saying. Early pictures of mastiffs show them with a variety of coat colours, many piebald, a colour that has prevailed through the years in our bulldogs and, through them, our Staffords. In 1413 Edward, second Duke of York, spoke about a dog of large proportions similar to a bulldog, and described him as "short-headed, pugnacious, and inclined to hang on to anything attacked."

The Old English Mastiff was the dog first used in England for bull-baiting, but their owners soon realised that the dog was too slow and cumbersome. Consequently, from this breed they developed a dog more slender, quicker, and lower to the ground, who retained the tenacity of his larger forebears. Crib and Rosa were perfect examples of bulldogs capable of doing the job they were bred for. In the next chapter we shall take a closer look at the development of dogs bred for sport in Britain.

Chapter Three

HISTORY OF THE FIGHTING DOG

Britain has a long and colourful sporting tradition, which grew out of the medieval spectacles of bull and bear baiting. Some people claim that our modern Stafford is a cross of bulldog and terrier, a perfect combination in dogs bred for sport.

TERRIERS

The name derives from the Latin 'terra' which means 'earth'. From primitive times man has hunted, and our earliest writers on the subject have acknowledged the terrier. This animal was so named because it was employed underground to force fox, badger and otter from their lairs. He was also kept for the purpose of killing rats, weasels and other vermin which infested the countryside when it was less cultivated than is the case today.

The first mention of the terrier is in the accounts of Edward I, in 1299-1300 : "Paid to William de Foxhunte, the King's huntsman of foxes in divers forest and parks for his own wages and the wages of his two boys to take care of the dogs – £9 3s"..... "Paid to the same for the keep of twelve dogs belonging to the King"......... "Paid to the same for the expense of a horse to carry the net....."

The next mention is by Edward, 2nd Duke of York, in his book *The Mayster of the Game* (1413). This was the first manuscript book of sport to be written in the English language, and in it he mentions "small curs that came to be terriers". One of the earliest pictorial representations of the terrier is given in Strutt's *Sports and Pastimes*. It consists of an engraving from a 14th century manuscript which depicts a dog, assisted by three men with spades, engaged in unearthing a fox. The colour of the dog is not ascertainable, nor can we be sure that it has been underground, for the fox is partly out of the hole, and the terrier is springing on his prey from rising ground immediately behind. A second terrier may possibly be out of sight in the earth. Two of the hunters are in the act of digging, while the third is blowing a horn. It is interesting that in the original engraving this terrier possesses a long, narrow head, not unlike that of a greyhound in shape. His tail is long and uncut; he is smooth-coated and has erect ears.

I have no doubt that this terrier record given to us by Strutt is the oldest upon which any reliance can be placed, so far as this country is concerned. Some may argue that this dog is not a terrier, but I believe it represents such a terrier as would be common at that time. It is a little bigger than the fox it is about to seize, and the general surroundings of the picture are in favour of this estimate of size.

King James I (VI of Scotland) was very fond of working his terriers, a sport he had learned as a boy in Scotland. James was so keen on his working dogs that he often neglected his regal duties in favour of watching bear and badger baiting, and he spent many a day digging out a fox from his earth. James must have inherited his love of sport from his mother, Mary Queen of Scots. On her

Alexander the Great's 'dog' killing the elephant and the lion.

The fight between the lion, Wallace, and the dogs, Tinker and Bell, at Warwick. Pierce Egan's Anecdotes, London 1827.

return to Scotland after her exile in France she took back with her "some hounds and terriers of great repute". These dogs soon became the main talking-point of the court as they were so good at their job. From this canine line came most of King James's best workers. King James had a rough-and-ready warrior look about him, and was sometimes called "the unkingly of Monarchs".

We know that James I and his son, Henry, witnessed the first lion-to-dog contest. The writer Stowe refers to this lion-baiting thus: "One of the dogs being put into the den was soon disabled by the lion, who took him by the head and neck and dragged him about. Another dog was then let loose, and served in the same manner, but the third, being put in immediately, seized the lion by the lip and held him for a considerable time, till, being severely torn by his claws, the dog was obliged to quit his hold, and the lion, greatly exhausted by the conflict, refused to renew the engagement, but, taking a sudden leap over the dogs, fled into the interior of his den. Two of the dogs died of their wounds, the third survived and was taken great care of by the prince, who said that he who had fought with the King of Beasts should never fight with an inferior creature."

BULL BAITING

Bull baiting was carried out by groups of people who mostly travelled from town to town with the same bull. Thus they gave local people in the 'sport' a chance to test their dogs. Most of the bulls became extremely scared, and were badly looked after by their handlers, but, at the same time, they grew very shrewd. Some would dig a hole with their horns, then put their nose in the hole, thus making the dog's job much harder. Usually the owners of such a bull would soon replace him. These same travellers were probably those who carried on the sport of bear baiting at fairs.

The name 'Bulldog' was commonly used to cover all types of dogs used for sport, i.e. bear baiting, badger baiting, dog fighting, rat killing, and of course, the original sport, bull baiting. The heavier type of bulldog was used for bull baiting, whereas the lighter type was used for rat killing. These two types were at either extreme from each other, one being in the region of 50 to 60 lbs, with the light type at 15 to 30 lbs. A more balanced medium type weighed in at 30 to 50 lbs.

Bulls attacked by Dogs: Sir Edwin Landseer, 1821.

The Bear Garden and Hope Theatre, 1616. This was London's most famous venue for bear baiting.

The Bear Garden and Hope Theatre 1616

BEAR BAITING

This barbarous sport had been in existence since Celtic days, but the most prolific period was in Tudor times, when London was the main focus of blood sports in Britain. A group of men known as Bearwards maintained a good supply of home-reared bears for the entertainment of the public at fairs, Saints' days, feast days and so forth. For a fee of ten shillings, locals were allowed to run their dogs against the bear, and handlers would waste no time in telling the people how good their chaps were in battle. The dog used in those days was a smaller type of Mastiff, who would hold on to the bear's nose or face with all the tenacity that he could muster. However, the dogs were usually torn to pieces by the teeth or claws of their far bigger adversary. Some of these bears became so famous that crowds of people would line the streets in towns where they were baited, just to get a glimpse of them. These contests very seldom saw the demise of the bear. Because of the hero-worship on the part of the crowd, the bait would usually proceed until most of the dogs were disposed of, or the bear was getting too much of a beating. Remember, there were sometimes five or six dogs attacking him at the same time. The handlers would pull the bear out, as he was very valuable and quite scarce. He then had to face the dogs at the next town's fair, probably only a couple of weeks away, and, in the meantime, his handlers had to repair his wounds.

The best-known venue for this sport was the aptly-named Beargarden at Southwark in London. This arena could hold over a thousand spectators. King Henry VIII was a great admirer of the sport and frequented it on many occasions. His daughter, Queen Elizabeth I, was also a keen participant, and was so fond of the bears that she gave names to most of the crowd's favourites. Bears like Sackerson, Tom, and Blind Robin were all among the favourites of Queen Bess. William Shakespeare also frequented The Garden, along with some of the aristocracy and foreign royalty. When the Queen died in 1603, the young Stuart king James VI of Scotland became James I of England. His great love of working dogs is well documented, as we have seen. He introduced an even smaller type of dog, more similar to the bulldog type that we see so much of in eighteenth century prints. James preferred bear baiting to bull baiting, probably due to the fact that they did not bait bulls in Scotland, but were more into badger baiting and hunting with hounds.

The Bear at Bay: Samuel Howitt, 1803.

Bear Baiting: Henry Alken, London 1820.

GAMECOCK FIGHTING AND THE PIT

The popularity of sport involving animals continued unabated throughout the 17th, 18th, and 19th centuries. There is a general belief that there was a switch from bull baiting to dog fighting. I am sorry to upset the applecart, but in fact most of the people involved in fighting dogs were those also interested in gamecock fighting. Fighting gamecocks was far more widespread than bull baiting, as it was much easier to transport cocks and dogs than to move a bull from one town to another. Because of the problems of transporting and housing the bull, most bull-runs took place at town fairs, which did not appear in towns too often. At fairs where bulls were baited, men also fought cocks and dogs, as well as staging bare-knuckle prizefights as sideshows. When the fairs were over, however, people would continue their local weekend contests, usually cockfighting and dog fighting.

The term 'pit' came from the gamecocks, but it was quite natural for the same name to be used for dog fighting, as on most occasions the dog used the same pit as the cocks. These dogs would also be used in rat killing contests — dogs like 'Billy' who wrote himself into the history books with his famous contest, killing 200 rats in one hour in the pit. Billy was described as a bulldog, but I think anybody can see from the pictures we have of him that in no way would his owners have thought of pitting him against a bull, for the simple reason that he was too small and light. Most dogs used on the bull would come in about 60 lbs, whereas Billy would have hit the scales about 30 lbs. Again we find the name 'pit' used for the rat killing, and, as I have said before, the gamecocks, fighting dogs and rat killing contests all took place at the same venue, with the same people taking part.

RAT PITS

The main aim in this sport was to have a dog who could kill rats more quickly than his rivals. As proof of the pudding, a specified number of rats would be loosed in the rat-pit. This was the same pit used for matches between dogs and monkeys, and similar forms of entertainment. It was square and boarded to a height of two or three or feet. In this square pit, pieces of metal had to be nailed at the top of the corners because rats were quite capable of climbing up these if not prevented.

A match would be made between two or more dogs to decide which was the most efficient at vermin destruction. Sometimes the match would decide which dog could kill the most rats in a specified time, and sometimes it would rest upon which could kill a specified number in the shortest time. The latter version was the most popular. When all was ready, stakes paid up and bets made, the rats were turned into the pits and the first dog brought along. He was held where he could see the quarry, his handler would wait for a favourable opportunity when the rats were placed as he wanted them, and would then drop his dog into the pit.

This signalled the start of the match, and the time-keeper began taking the time. The moment the dog touched the pit he started killing rats. He did not bother to pick them up and shake them, but simply gave each rat a hard bite and left him for the next. The dog used the pit well, and would slip quietly up the bunch, nipping them as they passed him, and he did not have much running about to do. If he was clever, he would work like a sheepdog, keeping a flock bunched to be brought out singly by nipping, and this continued until the last rat was caught. The dog was then picked up – a moment noted by the time-keeper as the end of that dog's performance.

At this point, the wrangles used to start. The side which owned the dog would claim all the rats were dead, and the side which had backed against the dog would say that some of them were still alive. A good terrier did not waste time shaking rats, but simply snapped them with one good grab which stopped the rat all right, but sometimes only broke his back, leaving a bit of a kick in him, though he could not crawl away. The method of deciding if he was technically alive was a bit rough and ready. He was picked up and put in a chalk circle about as big as a dinner plate. Someone who had backed against the dog, and was therefore interested in proving the rat alive, was given a piece of wood rather like a grocer's butter-pat. The rat's tail was then smacked sharply with the edge of this piece of wood, which must have been distinctly painful to any rats still physically alive, whether they were technically dead or not. If they were able to wriggle out of the chalk circle when thus 'encouraged', the verdict was that the dog had not killed them. If, on the other hand, they were too far gone to be persuaded to stir themselves, then they were technically dead, whatever they felt about it. What happened if they were alive depended upon the articles under which the match had been made. Sometimes it was stated that in the event of any rats remaining alive after the dog had been picked up, that dog was disqualified. At other matches he had to be put back in the pit, where he was re-timed until he had disposed of all his quarry.

Billy – The Rat Killer of Unrivalled Fame: Westminster Pit.

Aquatint G. Hunt.

Billy, the celebrated rat killing dog, London, 1823.

Occasionally, it would be stipulated that the dog could only have one bite at any rat and that, if he touched him after once putting him down, he lost the match. I have often wondered how these rat-pit terriers would work with ferrets. I imagine there would be complications at first, because they would not know where to stand so as to give the rats room to bolt clear of the holes, and the ferrets would be in great danger. Conversely, a dog used to ferrets would race into a bunch of rats like a bull in a china shop, scattering them all over the pit so that it would take longer to catch up with them than it would take a trained dog to kill them. That was how the rats were actually killed when a dog was put in the pit with them, and obviously a great many rats would be needed for a match since these specialist dogs could kill at a simply phenomenal rate.

For instance, I have an advertisement for a match at the Westminster pit on May 15th, 1825. Billy, the very famous dog mentioned earlier, was matched to kill 100 rats against a Kentish bitch who was almost equally famous. On this particular occasion, the official ratcatchers for the pit failed to provide the requisite 200 adult rats, so the match had to be declared 'no go'. The result with the rats available was that Billy disposed of 90 in seven and a half minutes, and the Kentish bitch killed 65 in eight minutes 45 seconds, which was a pretty good performance.

Another time, this same Billy was matched to kill 100 rats at a cockpit in Tufton Street in 12 minutes for £20 and bets. The floor of the pit was whitened to give him every chance, and he stopped the last one kicking within seven minutes 30 seconds. And so it goes on. I will not be dogmatic as to which dog captured the world record, for the contemporary accounts I have been able to trace were not complete, but this dog Billy once killed 100 in five minutes 30 seconds, which must have taken some beating. Certainly, no dog of his day could hold a candle to him, and when he was five or six years old, in June 1826, he killed his hundred in eight minutes 30 seconds, against a young dog which took 12 minutes and was still considered very good. I have been told that the greatest feat in the world was when a Liverpool dog killed 1,000 rats in less than an hour and three minutes, but there is no documentary proof of this feat. It would certainly have taken a dog with plenty of stamina and guts. I am sure that whoever owned such a dog must have been extremely proud of him.

In addition to straight matches over which dog could kill a certain quantity of rats quickest, irrespective of the weight of the dog, it was common to have handicaps based on weight. The champion Billy, who was white but for a patched head, weighed 27lbs, had fought in the dog pit and also baited bears in addition to his wonderful performance in the rat-pit. As time went on, however, rats became difficult to obtain in such numbers and it became fashionable to run handicaps. These were arranged so that the heavier the dog, the more rats he had to kill. Various handicaps were set, ranging from one rat added to a dog's quota for every 3lbs additional weight over his rival, to a rat for every pound. This arrangement was perhaps the favourite, and handicaps were frequently arranged in which each dog had to kill as many rats as there were pounds in his weight, the dog quickest in disposing of his quota being the winner. For instance, a 10lb dog would only have to kill ten rats, while Billy killed 27.

This put something of a premium on small dogs, and breeds were developed especially for this sport. The small, smooth, black and tan terriers of Manchester, and the rough type of Yorkshire terrier were particularly suitable. These little terriers came in weighing from 5lbs to 7lbs, and the fact that dogs so small were game enough to kill large rats at all always surprises me. That they could kill 20 in less than three minutes seems nothing short of miraculous.

Taken all in all, many of the Fancy regretted the passing of rat-pits. They did not die out as easily as other baiting sports, partly because they were less conspicuous, and partly because there was no general sympathy towards rats. There is, fortunately, still a possible alternative which lots of farmers and country folk employ when taking down the haystacks. They surround the stack with 1-inch wire netting 3ft high and, as they get near the bottom, you can see the rats moving about it. The farmers then introduce the dogs. In one afternoon you can see as many as 50 to 100 rats being killed by sheepdogs and terriers alike – and then go home and dream about the dogs that could kill as many in five or ten minutes.

DOG FIGHTING

For centuries, men who frequented bull rings and bear pits had also enjoyed watching two dogs fight. There is nothing very complicated in the rules of dog fighting, and the important thing is not so much to kill the other dog as to be game enough to try. In the days when the sport was still legal and at the height of its popularity — between 1780 and 1835 — dog fights were a regular part of the sport on offer at such famous centres of attraction as London's Westminster pit, not to mention Charley's (the Cockpit), Duck Lane pit and many others. As I have made clear, these arenas were also used for contests between various strange combatants, dogs against monkeys, dogs against raccoons and so forth.

*Badger baiting:
Henry Alken,
London 1824.*

*Dog fighting in
action: Henry
Alken, London,
1820.*

*Dog Fight:
Henry Alken,
London 1824.*

The pit itself was roughly 12-18 feet across, with a boarded surround about three feet high, over which spectators could watch. Each dog was handled by his seconds and, after preliminary formalities concerning the stakes had been completed, each dog was weighed in the pit. So much does sheer weight count that matches were rarely made at more than a maximum excess of one pound over the stipulated weight. If a match were made to be fought at 38lbs, give or take a pound, a dog coming to the pit so much as a few ounces over 39lbs would be disqualified and the stakes forfeited.

Two good dogs would sometimes take as much as two hours to decide which was the better, and rarely less than 25 or 30 minutes. However good a dog was known to be, nobody but a fool would match him against anything but a "cur" outside his weight class. The men who kept fighting terriers considered all breeds "curs" if they were not game in the pit. There was often a good deal of trickery of the lowest sort employed to ensure that a particular dog should win. He would be rubbed over with acid, pickle or pepper, anything to discourage his opponent from biting him. To avoid this deception, a common butt of water was provided, from which both dogs had to be washed, or sometimes milk was used to "kill" the acid. As an additional precaution each Setter was allowed to "taste" or lick his opponent's dog, both before and after fighting, to satisfy himself that nothing pernicious had been used.

When the preliminaries had been completed, a coin was tossed to decide which dog should "scratch" first. They went to opposite corners of the pit, where the Second held his dog between his knees so that the other dog got a fair, unobstructed view of his opponent's head. On a word from the referee, the dog which had to "scratch" first was liberated, and had to go across the pit to attack his opponent. A line drawn across the centre of the pit was known as "the scratch", and the opposing dog could not be loosed until his attacker had crossed this line. When he had crossed "the scratch", the second Setter could loose his dog whenever he liked and judgement at this moment won or lost many battles. If a Setter thought his opponent was not fast or aggressive, he might risk holding his dog quite still and if the other dog did not begin to fight, he automatically lost the battle. If his judgement was wrong and the other dog did fight at once, the dog which had been held still until his opponent caught hold of him where he wanted to, was at an obvious disadvantage. If, on the other hand, the Setter thought his opponent was pretty fast, his obvious tactic was to loose his dog the moment the other dog crossed "the scratch", so that they met on equal terms. Sometimes a Setter opposed to a fast dog would hold his until the last moment and slip him to one side, so that the other dog rushed harmlessly by. The Setter then loosed his dog in the hope he could get a hold before his adversary had recovered his balance. This was an obvious case of "not showing his dog's head fair to scratch", and should have been penalised by the referee.

When both dogs started to fight, and not before, the Setters could leave the pit and, though they could encourage their own dogs, they were forbidden to speak to their opponent's dog. Neither dog could be touched again until both stopped fighting, which would eventually happen when they were short of wind or otherwise exhausted. When this happened, either Setter could pick up his dog. If the opposing dog still showed fight, he was obliged to put it down again and allow them to continue. If he could get his dog away unmolested, he took him to his corner and the round expired. One minute was allowed for sponging down and making ready for the next round. The referee gave warning after 50 seconds, so that both should be ready when the minute was up. This time the dog who "scratched" first was held while his opponent came to "scratch" and the battle went on again, for no set time, but until both dogs "faulted" again. Sometimes, these rounds lasted for 20 minutes or more. Towards the end of a battle, when both dogs were becoming weak or short of breath, there might only be a few minutes between "scratches". A battle of an hour or more might have 20 "scratches", or one dog might be killed in the first "scratch". It was very like the old prizefight ring rules, where men did not fight for a stipulated time, but until one fell to the ground.

The battle was lost by the first dog to fail to come to "scratch" on his turn. It was not necessarily the dog which killed his opponent who won, but the dog which proved most game. If a dog was killed in the pit, the other had to stay at him for ten minutes at least and could still not be handled by his Setter till he faulted. Then he was taken to his corner. If it was the dead dog's turn to "scratch", the battle was automatically lost, but if it was the live dog's turn and he did not "scratch", he lost the battle although he had killed his opponent.

Chapter Four

CREATION OF THE BREED

As we have seen, the cockfighting fraternity was equally interested in dogs, and during the Regency period many of its foremost members became involved in canine breeding. Among the leading 'cockers' of this era were the Duke of Northumberland, the Duke of Hamilton, the Earl of Mexburgh, Lord Vere, Lord Lonsdale and Lord Derby. In 1817, the Grand Duke Nicholas of Russia, accompanied by the Duke of Devonshire, the Russian Ambassador, Sir William Congreve, Baron Michola, General Kutusoff and others, went to the Cockpit Royal and spent an hour and a half watching five battles, in which the Russian visitors were greatly interested, never before having seen a cock fight. They were later taken to watch two dog fights, which they also found fascinating.

King George IV, when Prince Regent, was exceedingly fond of the cockpit. It is said that on one occasion he and the Duke of York lost so much money over a "main" that they had to send out to a neighbouring tavern to borrow what was necessary to pay their losses. The keeper of the tavern was given a free licence in recognition of this service to Royalty.

The 12th Earl of Derby was recognised as the foremost cocker of his time, holding his own with all the top pit men of the day. He was the last English peer to play a prominent part in the sport. Lord Derby succeeded to the title at the age of twelve and came of age in 1775. Throughout his life he was devoted to cocking, and horseracing, and was, with his friend the Duke of Hamilton, a great patron of the dog-fighting pits. On many occasions, both he and the Duke lost and won large wagers on their horses, cocks and fighting dogs. Sometimes these wagers would go as high as 2,000 or 3,000 guineas. The contests mostly took place at race meetings, and Lord Derby's favourite meetings were Preston and Liverpool, both near his Knowsley estate. He owed his subsequent successful career to Paul Potter, one of the most skilful trainers and feeders of the time. The first time Lord Derby is mentioned for the success he was having was in the *Racing Calendar* for 1790.

Cock bags were usually made of linen, but Lord Derby's were of silk, with a fighting cock embroidered in his colours. His fighting dogs had the the best English leather collars, embroidered with the dog's name in silver. When he died at the age of 82, in 1834, all his birds, spurs, bags, fighting dogs and fighting equipment became the property of the younger Potter, son of Paul Potter. Young Potter kept a tavern at Hartlebury.

THE DUKE OF HAMILTON

In the early days of the development of fighting dogs, after the demise of the 'buildog', many areas created their own type. In the north the heavier dog was preferred, while in the Midlands they liked the smaller ones. People from all walks of life were involved in the Fancy, from wealthy

*The Duke of
Hamilton's
breed, circa
1780.*

*The Duke of
Hamilton, circa
1790.*

aristocrats to innkeepers, chainmakers, miners, weavers, prizefighters, rat catchers and many others.

   Probably the most important figure, who was accepted nationwide as the father of the 'new breed' of fighting dog, was the Duke of Hamilton. His Grace spent lots of time and money perfecting this breed, and he frequented all the known pits with his dogs, who were seldom beaten. He was inundated with enquiries from other titled folk keen to acquire some of his young stock, for to own one of the Duke of Hamilton's breed was a feather in the cap of anyone in the Fancy. His Grace was held in very high esteem, and was accepted as the doyen of the fighting dog. On one occasion, while he was visiting his club in London, one of his friends turned to him as they entered the door and said:"Look, your Grace, one of your 'breed' with that young beau." It was quite a common sight to see one of the young gentry of the day walking out with one of the Duke of Hamilton's breed. The Duke was a well-known sporting gentleman, and his racehorses were well to the fore in all the big races. He often frequented the cellars in some well-known inns in Glasgow and the surrounding areas, like the Beehive in Kirkintilloch, the Zebra and the Zaracin's Head in Glasgow.

   The Prince of Wales, later George IV, was a personal friend of the Duke of Hamilton and a great

The Prince of Wales, King George IV.

George Stubbs, 1790.

admirer of gamecocks, dogfighting, and bare-knuckle bouts. He was a prince who enjoyed gambling, drinking, furious riding and behaving, in short, like the great majority of his contemporaries. The wisdom of the writer Horace Walpole was evident when he wrote of the young prince: "As I too am always partial to youth – having not at least the spleen of age – I make the greatest allowance for inexperience and moral passions." We know that the Prince possessed at least two of the Duke of Hamilton's breed thanks to a portrait, painted about 1790, by the artist George Townley Stubbs. It shows the sporting prince on horseback, accompanied by two canine outriders.

WASP, CHILD, BILLY AND TYGER

These four fighting dogs were from the kennel of His Grace, the Duke of Hamilton. As a young man he took a great interest in fighting dogs about 1770, then developed his own fighting strain from the lighter and quicker bulldog of the day that he also kept. In H.B. Chalon's painting of Wasp, Child and Billy, owned at that time by Mr Henry Boynton who acquired them after the death of the Duke of Hamilton in 1801, you can see that their likeness in type to the present-day Stafford is remarkable. The bitch, Tyger, is without doubt a perfect example of the first nationally-accepted fighting dog referred to by name as the Duke of Hamilton's breed. His Grace was so fond of this animal that he had a painting commissioned of himself with Tyger in the 'make ready' position.

In these examples we have the first named "breed" within this type of dog. How his Grace perfected this breed is a question I have often asked myself. We know that he kept a number of the old-fashioned type of bulldogs with their longer legs, short backs and pump-handle tails. I think what he did was to select the racier ones, who were faster and could change their grip quickly to get a better hold. These attributes, along with the tenacity of the old bulldog, gave his "breed" the advantage over other fighting dogs, who were of much more dubious breeding, and did not really stand much chance against this streamlined dog.

Wasp, Child and Billy by H.B. Chanlon. These dogs show a remarkable likeness to the present-day Stafford.

APPEARANCE IN ART

Theories abound about the exact development of the Staffordshire Bull Terrier from cross Terrier/Bulldog to old-style Bulldog and so on. However, we can get a good idea of what went on from studying the depiction of the breed in works of art. Some of the prominent artists of the period 1780-1830 painted dogs owned by aristocrats and other wealthy people. Quite a few of these dogs were the forebears of our modern Staffordshire Bull Terrier. This half-century was rich in all types of art, and we must be grateful so many paintings of bulldogs were done. It gives us a great insight into the beginnings of the breed and the purpose for which it was created. Henry Alken was the most famous artist of that era for paintings of badger baiting, bull and bear baiting, dog fighting and rat killing. All of these subjects, in full colour, appeared in Alken's *National Sports of Great Britain 1820.*

The picture of Crib and Rosa shows dogs more like our present-day Staffords. Their outline, their long straight legs, and pump-handle tails are all the traits that we have come to expect of our modern breed. I am very strongly of the opinion, along with the late Nat Cairns, Joe Dunn and others, that their type of Bulldog from the early 19th century has continued to the present day. The only thing we have done is to change the name and compile a breed standard that describes the Stafford we know today.

Paintings and prints showing the typical bulldog of circa 1808-1820, such as the one of Crib and Rosa by Abraham Cooper (1816), leave me with no doubt that this type of dog is the direct ancestor of our Staffordshire Bull Terrier. The bitch Rosa is far more like a present-day Stafford than she is like the present-day bulldog. However, this is the bitch that Bulldog enthusiasts used as an ideal Bulldog when they drew up their breed standard for the Kennel Club.

The painter Stubbs captured the Bull Terrier in a pose that we would be proud of in a show ring today. That "Here I am, look at me!" cockiness has never left the breed from those early days right through to the present, and the painting was done about 1812. In another painting by H.B. Chalon (circa 1808) of Wasp, Child and Billy, three of the Duke of Hamilton's breed previously

The early Stafford type. Note the undershot jaw and cropped ears.

Crib and Rosa: A detail from a hand-coloured engraving, after a painting by A. Cooper, London, 1817. The bitch, Rosa, was used as an 'ideal' by the Bulldog fraternity when they were drawing up a Breed Standard.

Bull-and-Terrier by George Stubbs 1812.

mentioned, the bitch Wasp bears a very strong resemblance to the Bull Terrier that Stubbs painted. In fact, I would go so far as to say that Wasp and Stubbs' Bull Terrier are probably mother and son, the likeness is so close. Using computer techniques, we built up a picture of Wasp standing up and compared it to the Bull Terrier painted by Stubbs. Looking at it, I came to the conclusion that they must be closely related, as the resemblance is so startling.

James B. Morrison's Blue Paul dog, called 'Paul'. The Blue Paul is thought to be behind the breeding of the American Staffordshire Terrier and the Pit Bull Terrier. It could also be behind the breeding of Staffordshire Bull Terriers.

THE BLUE PAUL

The Blue Paul was a dog, known for his pluck and gameness, from the Kirkintilloch area near Glasgow in Scotland. This dog was bred from an Irish Blue (later called the Kerry Blue) and a white dog of the Duke of Hamilton's breed belonging to a Dr Robertson of Campsie. A certain Mr Shaw, landlord of the Beehive Inn, along with some of the Fancy in the town, successfully developed this new breed, and by 1830 they were sought after with great enthusiasm by people from all parts of the world. Breeds such as Pit-Bull Terriers and American Staffordshire Terriers have this breed behind them and, according to some sources, the Blue Paul is also behind Staffordshire Bull Terriers.

Until recently, the history of the Blue Paul was shrouded in mystery. Stories abounded: pirates like Paul Jones were involved with the breed; the dogs were upwards of 60 lbs; and so on. However, in all my years of researching this breed I have found no factual evidence to link the Blue Paul with Paul Jones or any other mythical tales. What we do know is that an Infantry Regiment, the 91st Foot, had returned to Dover from the Peninsular Wars. They were transferred to Cork in Southern Ireland, and on Christmas Day 1816 made their way to Dublin, to put down an uprising of 'Whiteboys', radicals involved with the Roman Catholic community. After successfully completing their mission, the soldiers were disbanded. A year later, the British government decided that another radical group, the Weavers of Central Scotland, had to be taught a lesson, and the regiment was reformed. This time more Irish foot soldiers were attached to them, but the officers were all Scotsmen. The Commanding Officer was a Colonel McNeil of Oronsay (an island off the west coast of Scotland).

The McNeils were well known for their sporting dogs. In fact, during Colonel McNeil's stay in Ireland he became very friendly with the 'Omohow' – the Lord of Kerry – who had a very famous strain of Irish Wolfhounds similar to a Mastiff. One of these dogs was mated to the McNeil's Deerhound or Staghound, as it was commonly known in those days. This cross changed the Wolfhound to more or less the type of dog that we know today as the Irish Wolfhound. This pleased the Omohow of Kerry so much that he let McNeil have one of his 'Irish Blue' bitches, renowned in Ireland at that time for its fighting ability. When Colonel McNeil's regiment was posted back to Glasgow and Paisley, he brought with him his Irish Blue bitch. After 1820, when the regiment was very quickly moved to Jamaica, all pets and livestock were left behind. The Weavers' insurrection had ended with the martyrs being hanged at Glasgow Green. The Colonel's Irish Blue bitch was left with friends in the Kirkintilloch area, but she was such a handful that the local Fancy acquired her for her fighting abilities. They mated her to Dr Robertson's white dog from the Duke of Hamilton's breed and the story of the notorious Blue Paul began.

Nobody has known more about the Blue Paul than Mr J.B. Morrison, the renowned All-rounder and Championship show judge from Greenock. Mr Morrison was one of Scotland's foremost authorities on Terriers and also a founder member and first chairman of the Terrier Club of Scotland. He ran a tea and wine importing business in Greenock, was well over six feet tall and always immaculately dressed. He could be seen every morning walking from his house in upper Greenock to his offices in the lower part of the town, very splendid with his top-hat and silver-topped cane. Mr Morrison owned 'Paul', the best Blue Paul in Scotland, showing this particular dog at the Kelvin Hall in Glasgow and winning with some ease.

We know that the Blue Paul appeared in great strength in the Bishopton, Port Glasgow and Greenock areas up until about 1910, and we know that the travelling people of Ireland took these dogs back with them to their homeland. Until only two years ago, no more was known about them, but my great interest in this breed of dog led me to talk to Kerry Blue enthusiasts (the modern name for the Irish Blue). One particularly good source was the famous 'Granemore Kerry Blue' man, Malachy McGeown, who originally came from Armagh in Northern Ireland and now lives in Chorley, Lancashire, in England. Malachy told me that when he was only a boy, his father used to frequent the local pub, where one evening two or three travelling people turned up. With them was a fairly large dog, blue in colour, with a very powerful head. His father took a great liking to this dog, and asked the gipsy if he could buy him. Eventually the gipsy said yes, and his father acquired the dog. He told his family that its name was Dan and it was a breed called Blue Paul. Dan lived with the family for ten years and terrorised every other dog in the neighbourhood.

CONTEMPORARY EVIDENCE

The interesting thing about this story is that it happened in the 1940s, so here we have the Blue Paul turning up about thirty years after the breed was presumed extinct. Also we are talking about only one dog that Malachy knew. I am quite sure that travelling people in the north-west of Ireland must have had more of these dogs in their encampments. In fact, as recently as 1993 I was used as an expert witness in the first 'Dangerous Dogs' case in Ireland. During my stay there, I took some time out to visit the glens and small villages to talk to old men who had travelling people and gipsy breeding in them. After many miles and introductions to the right people, whispers here, and a nod and a wink there, I was at last introduced to 'Willie', the doyen of the working dog fraternity in Northern Ireland.

Willie told me that – wait for it! – the Blue Paul was still alive and kicking, but there were not too many left. You can imagine my next question. Would it be possible for me to see one? Willie looked at me and then at the friend who had introduced us, and with what I would call a very forceful reply he said: "You will see nothing, boy, until we have checked you out!" One major rule I had forgotten in my eagerness to see the dogs was never to ask these people for anything – let them offer! My heart sank — all my years of research into the breed was going out of the window! This fraternity of clandestine people are ultra-careful as to who is allowed to see their dogs – or birds for that matter. Thankfully, Willie then looked at me again and said: "The next time you come over to Ireland, boy, I'll have something for you to see." I am eagerly awaiting my invitation. If the dogs in Ireland are from the original stock last seen in the Greenock area and are indeed Blue Pauls, many questions will be answered. It would be great to know that the dog which was developed in Scotland long before either the Bull Terrier or our Staffordshire Bull Terrier existed has not been lost for ever.

Mr Morrison insists that, contrary to what we have been told, the Blue Paul very seldom weighed 60lbs, and was nearer the 45lb mark. Knowing how hard it is for other breeds, such as Whippets and Great Danes, to keep their blue colour consistent, I can well understand why, in the early days, breeders of the Blue Paul found it so hard to keep the colour true. I am sure they did not understand genetics in the way that the foremost breeders of this colour do nowadays. Their main aim was to retain the fighting ability of the dog, and by doing this, unbeknown to them, they started to lose the original colour. This is why later writers said indiscriminate breeding had led to the loss of the colour. This was not actually the case at all. The dogs were as much Blue Pauls as those who were actually blue in colour, the only difference being that, for some unknown reason, the blue-coloured animals were more aloof, and were also loners and more ferocious than their litter brothers and sisters. If only they had realised that by using the fawn and black brindles they could have bred more blue pups in their litters!

Here is Mr Morrison's description of the Blue Paul: "In the hope that the description of this breed of dog, whose numbers are unfortunately dwindling, may not only interest some of the younger fanciers, but awaken pleasant reminiscences in the memories of a few of those who have had their day, I will give a brief account of the dog as I know him.

"The general appearance of the Blue Paul is that of a smooth-coated, powerfully-built, cobby dog, about 45lbs and about 20 inches at the shoulder, more after the style of the bulldog than any other of the present fancy. Head large, forehead flat, muzzle short and square, nose black, large and broad, but not receding like that of the bulldog. Jaws and lips even, with no overhanging flews, a slight stop between the eyes, which are dark hazel, neither sunk nor prominent, and with no white or haw seen. Ears small and thin, set on high, and invariably cropped, the face not wrinkled, but eyebrows contracted or knit, and, as the dog lowered one side of his head when at attention, this, with the contraction of the eyebrows, gave the dog a peculiarly intelligent but comical look. In fact, there was an expression in the face of the Blue Paul that I never saw in any other breed, and I have frequently recognised this look in cross-bred dogs from this peculiarity. Body round and well ribbed up, back short, broad, and muscular, but not roached, chest very wide and deep, tail set on low devoid of fringe, and rather drooping in carriage, never rising above the back. The dog stands straight and firmly on his legs, forelegs very stout and muscular, showing no curve, with elbows standing in towards the ribs, hind legs and thighs very thick, strong and well-furnished with muscle. The colour was that peculiar shade of dark blue we see occasionally in greyhounds. These points went to make up a dog that arrested the attention of a fancier, at once producing, as they did, a combination of great strength and beauty.

"The Blue Paul is a dog full of character. For pluck, courage and endurance he was unapproachable, and if not particularly quarrelsome, he certainly feared no foe, and required no coaxing to do battle when asked, his nimbleness and tenacity making him a dangerous adversary. The most remarkable feature of his character is his rare intelligence and wonderful display of what I can only call reason. I have long believed that at least some of the lower animals are endowed not only with that singular gift, instinct, but with the higher faculty of reason, and those who have been the fortunate possessor of a Blue Paul will bear me out in saying that this dog's reason was almost human."

"THE BLUE PAUL AND THE MONKEY"
This poem by Kenneth Robertson gives an insight into the popularity of the Blue Paul in the area of his birth. The verses were written in the old Scottish language, but for the convenience of English-speaking readers we have translated them.

> A night into a pub there came
> A man with a dog of fighting fame,
> A man who looked the same,
> Saying he had bought it.
> An organ grinder sitting quiet
> Listening to the man relate,
> The tale of some dog's hapless fate
> That once had fought it.
>
> At length says grinder: "Listen mate,
> "No doubt your dog is all you state,
> "But I'll match him against 'Pawky Pate'
> "My wee pet monkey."
> The owner of the fighting dog
> With laughter choking over his fag,
> Says he: "Now I have met many a fool,
> "But you're a donkey."
>
> "Now, maybe if you had brought a bear
> "Instead of that wee monkey there
> "I would fancy that your chance was fair.
> "But what's your bet?"
> Says organ grinder: "I've five pounds
> "And if you'd like to raise the bid
> "I have a stone of coppers I'll get rid
> "That, too, you will get."
>
> The match created quite a stir
> Amongst the men there drinking beer.
> They stepped back a place to clear
> And watch the battle.
> Wee Pate was set down on the floor
> The dog, unleashed, already there.
> Expectant tenseness in the air,
> No glass did rattle.
>
> The fight was on, the scene was set,
> Each man had settled on his bet.
> The organ grinder for his pet

Showed no great fear.
"Seize him", hissed the doggy man,
But Pate had formed another plan,
For as at him the Blue Paul ran,
Pate jumped clear.

The Blue Paul's head crashed off the wall,
While back from him Wee Pate did draw.
The Blue Paul turned, and when Pate saw
He attacked quick.
Again, he was that wee bit late
To catch elusive monkey Pate,
For Pate jumped up onto a seat,
And seized a stick.

The organ grinder had taken care
To see that a stick was lying there.
Says grinder, "Now on", and this is where
Pate makes attack.
Again, wee Pate was far too quick
To fall for such a clumsy trick,
Over that dog's head he brought the stick
A hefty crack.

And then he jumped back off the floor
Up on to a handy chair,
Then took another jump from there
On that dog's back.
That poor misbegotten whelp's
Ferocious growls now turned to yelps
Whenever Wee Pate took a skelp
At head or side.

And how that crowd did laugh and roar.
Such fun they had never had before
As Blue Paul made for out the door
With Pate astride.

The home of that unhappy Paul
Lay a bit beyond the toll,
Where dwelt an old short-sighted soul
Of female sex.
It was just an hour of gloaming gray,
When Pate and Blue Paul passed her way.
She spotted them and shouted: "Hey,
"Come back and pay your tax!"

Her old eye must have magnified,
A man on horseback thought she spied
For loudly after them she cried:
"You have gone over far.
"Come back," she cried, "And pay your toll,
"I know you fine, you ugly soul,
"Wee Jock McNutty from the hole,
"That's who you are!"

THE STAFFORD TODAY

The Staffordshire Bull Terrier that we know today has not changed to any great extent from the dog that was developed 200 years ago by the Duke of Hamilton, apart from the fact that we now have a breed standard to adhere to. All the written history and paintings from that period give us evidence to believe this to be so. The Duke of Hamilton was involved in the Fancy from 1775 until his death in 1801. After he died, his breed was extensively used as an anchor breed in producing the dog that we know today.

Some people argue that the breed's development is hidden somewhere in the 18th century. I personally think that the reason for this belief is that no one kept written records of the mating of their individual dogs – that is, until we discovered that the Duke of Hamilton kept a comprehensive record of all his matings. The fact that his breed can be seen so strongly in our Stafford today proves how close his breeding programme really was. It must have been an inbred line to have been so dominant. His Grace was using not just the classic theory that great fighters put together produce proven dogs of courage, but he was also using the more scientific method of brother to sister, mother to son, father to daughter, and by doing so was able to reach his goal a lot quicker than other members of the dogfighting fraternity. The flashy markings from his dogs can be seen in our present-day breed, as well as the smoothness of coat we are so used to seeing and feeling.

Men from the Black Country had their own ideas and bred dogs to their own liking, as did the men from Newcastle, Manchester, London and so forth. Even up until registration by the Kennel Club in 1935, Black Country men did not have a true, written authenticated family tree for their dogs, although the most important thing – 'type' – was retained, even if most dog breeders lacked imagination in picking names for their charges. Names such as Madman, Puss, Mell, and Billy, were quite often repeated time after time. No wonder they did not bother with pedigrees, as they would have been confusing, to say the least. The first dog of the Staffordshire Bull Terrier type (shown as a Bull Terrier) was called Como II, and belonged to Mr E.H. Adcock of Epsom. It was a brindled dog of pretty good shape, with a heavier body and a short Stafford-type head. Mr Adcock's endeavours to perpetuate the strain did not, however, meet with the universal approval of show-going people.

DOG FIGHTING TODAY

Although there was no definite type of fighting dog at the turn of the 18th century, the Duke of Hamilton's breed was soon developed for this specific purpose, At a later date, as we have seen, it became known as the Staffordshire Bull Terrier. Dog fighting has become illegal since the days of the Westminster pit, and by the middle of the last century fighting had to be arranged surreptitiously. It was very popular in London until the beginning of this century and a little has been carried on in the Midlands at intervals since then. The first consideration in getting a dog fighting-fit was to get his wind right and to remove all surplus fat. He had to be given constant hard exercise to get him muscled up and in extremely hard condition. This was best achieved by giving small quantities of high nutrition food, with an absence of starchy food, during his training. The jelly from cow's heel and an adequate supply of fresh green food formed a good basis. Plenty of hard walking on a lead with a wide collar meant that he could pull and helped to strengthen his back and loin muscles. An old motor tyre or other piece of old rubber, suspended so that he could jump, catch hold and shake himself about on it, was simply vital.

The damage that a fighting dog could do was not so much by the sheer force of his bite, but by the shaking when he got hold, and his neck and back muscles were essential for this. Plenty of running and jumping for a ball that bounced well strengthened all the muscles he used in turning and twisting and produced the required agility. When he was thoroughly fit, the fighting dog was the very personification of energy. His coat glistened until it seemed to exude good health, his eyes were bright and there was a rippling mass of muscles stretching from his cheeks, down his neck and shoulders to his loin. He danced like a boxer in the ring, and once a dog tried fighting, he would attack anything that moved from a mouse to a mule.

Police interference has increased until all organised dog fighting in this country has now been very nearly stamped out. Unfortunately, there is still a hard core of game terrier people who, because of their gambling instincts, will always want to feel the adrenaline flowing and the "buzz" of the fight. Many successful dogs were shipped to America, along with Blue Pauls, where they became known as Pit Bull Terriers. At present, there is still an American periodical devoted to this breed and its activities, and enthusiasts hold what they call "Pit Bull conventions".

Despite the illegality of the Sport in this country, it has always been carried on spasmodically to a small extent. Periodically, the press write of "orgies" of dog fighting alleged to have been carried on for fabulous stakes, usually behind locked doors in the presence of beautiful women gambling away their fortunes or their honour on the gory results of some battle! In reality, the reports are usually an elaboration woven round scraps of conversation overheard through the fumes in some pub or bar. The battle which may or may not have been described will have taken place in some cellar, pigsty or barn in the presence of three to five men, all of whom are intimately known to each other. They never fight in the same place twice, and rarely ever keep the dogs they fight, usually collecting them for the occasion from men who train them and they will be busily engaged in securing a watertight alibi elsewhere.

The whole proceedings will be notable more for sordidness than glamour. Nobody but the people concerned know when or where the next "job" is coming off, and the sum total of battles fought is very small, to keep chances of detection negligible. The dogs themselves take to fighting like a Spaniel to a gun, and their absolute craziness to get at each other has to be seen to be believed. The men who watch them are of an equally unusual type. That they have little imagination goes without saying, but I find it surprising that a low percentage appear to take sadistic delight in their battling dogs. They almost worship the quality of aggressive gameness, and are usually as willing to fight each other as to watch the animals.

Chapter Five

CHOOSING A STAFFORD

Before you purchase a Staffordshire Bull Terrier, there are several questions you should ask yourself begin looking at litters of puppies. If the prospective purchaser knows what they are looking for, it will save a lot of wasted time, effort, and possible disappointment. All humans are different, and the same is true of dogs. Ideally, you should choose a dog that will suit your own personality. However, if you are buying a dog for the family, you must put your children's needs first and select a dog that will thrive in the family set-up.

THE FAMILY STAFFORD
If you are buying a Stafford for your children, it is essential that the dog should be regarded as a playmate, rather than a plaything. If you do not think that your children are capable of respecting a living creature, then it would be better for the children – and for the dog – if you bought a mechanical toy. However, if your children can be taught to respect the dog, there is much mutual benefit to be gained from the relationship. Your children will learn to be more caring and responsible, and the dog will enjoy the fun and companionship of playing with children.

Staffordshire Bull Terriers are well-known for their affectionate nature, particularly with children. However, children must be taught to respect the rights of another living creature, and adults must be prepared to supervise interactions between dog and child.

The puppy who will suit a family is a strong, friendly, happy-go-lucky sort, with as few inhibitions as possible. It is then your responsibility to guide the puppy's development so that the adult fulfils all the early potential.

THE SHOW STAFFORD

If you are planning to show your Stafford, you are looking for a puppy who will correspond as closely to the national Kennel Club Breed Standard as an adult. Neither the puppy nor the parents should have any outstanding faults – although it is important to remember that there is no such thing as a perfect dog: if there was, the breeder would certainly not sell it! You must also bear in mind that a Stafford bought for show purposes or for breeding will be more expensive than the puppy who is bought purely as a companion.

In order to buy a show-quality Stafford, you will need to acquire a thorough knowledge of the leading breeders. The best way to do this is to go to some shows where Staffords are being judged. This will give you the opportunity to find out the type of dog you are attracted to, and to find out which lines are most successful in the show ring. You can then track down individual breeders by looking the dogs up in the show catalogue, where both owners and breeders are listed. You will then need to research pedigrees going back over several generations, so that you have an in-depth knowledge of the type of Stafford a particular line produces.

CHOOSING A BREEDER

Whether you are buying a show Stafford or a companion Stafford, it is essential to find a caring, responsible breeder, who has a reputation for selling good, sound dogs. Do not be misled by sales talk or kennel advertisements. The priority is to find a kennel who consistently produces dogs of a sound temperament and provides good after-sales service. If you are looking for a show Stafford, do not rush to the kennel that has just done a lot of winning. It is better to go to a kennel which has consistently produced Staffords of show quality over a number of years.

The best course of action is to contact your national Kennel Club for a list of breed clubs in your area. If you get in touch with the club secretary, you will probably be given a list of reputable breeders; the secretary may even know which breeders have puppies currently available. Do not make the mistake of rushing off to a kennel without making prior arrangements. Breeders are busy people, and most kennels are run to a set routine. Book a time when the breeder will be free to talk to you, and, hopefully, you will be asked to come when the puppies are likely to be at their liveliest.

Stafford breeders share one thing in common – and that is a great love for their dogs. Therefore, do not be surprised if the breeder asks you searching questions about your home and lifestyle. It is all too easy to assume that 'the customer is king', and it is only a matter of stating what you want. However, this is not the case when you are dealing with livestock. A breeder does not *have* to sell a puppy to you – and the majority will not do so if they feel you cannot provide a good, caring home.

PUPPY OR ADULT?

The majority of purchasers are keen to buy a puppy, but there are circumstances where an adult may be more suitable, either for domestic considerations, or because a particular dog will fit in with your breeding or showing programme. Obviously, a puppy will adapt more quickly to a change of home – although, in my experience, Staffords are probably the most adaptable of all breeds when it comes to a change of home. In the old days, their ancestors had to move from one home to another, and so I believe this ability to settle in has been bred into them. The advantage of

Solid Man of Dumbriton (2CCs, 3 RCCs).

The majority of pet owners decide to buy a puppy rather than an adult, but there are situations where an adult may be more suitable. Staffords are among the most adaptable of all breeds, and, hopefully, the adult Stafford will be quick to settle into a new home.

buying an adult is that you know what you are getting, in terms of both personality and appearance.

COLOUR
With Staffords, there is a full range of colours to choose from, and so your choice will be based on your own particular preference. I have often been asked whether there is a difference in personality between Staffords of different colours, and I can honestly say that I have never detected it. In most cases, you will be attracted to the personality of a puppy, and the colour becomes a secondary consideration. Contrary to common belief, white Staffords are not particularly hard to keep clean; the amount of effort involved in keeping the coat in good order is roughly the same for all colours. The old adage "a good horse is a good colour" applies equally to dogs, and whatever you select, the colour should be strong, rich and true.

STAFFORD COLOURS

Dutch, Belg. Lux. Int. Ch. Bethane Beau Brummel: The red Stafford should be rich in colour, and a black mask on the face is desirable.

Ch. Kablice Midnight Caller: The black Stafford may be solid black or with white markings.

Ch. Quarterflash War Squaw: Markings can be split between two colours, illustrated by this top-winning black and white Stafford.

David Dalton.

Little Brindle Bess of Bethane: The brindle colour can be of any shade, with or without white markings.

Dutch. Germ. Int. and World Ch. Tenacious Just Kidding: The white strain was introduced into the breeding of Staffordshire Bull Terriers at an early stage of the breed's development.

Ch. White of Morn: These distinctive markings on a solid white background contribute to the impressive appearance.

Raymond.

MALE OR FEMALE?

Personally, I do not believe there is much difference in personality between male and female Staffords, so, again, your choice will be based on your own preference. Males and females are equally affectionate, gentle and intelligent. A bitch comes into season every six months for a period of two to three weeks, and during this time you will have to keep her away from males. Some people find this a bit of a nuisance, particularly if you live in an urban environment where neighbouring dogs may be on the prowl. Conversely, some people find that bitches are easier to house-train than males.

You may decide to have your bitch spayed in order to overcome the problems of coping with her seasonal cycle. If this is done just before or just after her first season, and the operation is carried out by a competent veterinary surgeon, there will be no ill-effects on your bitch. The operation will not affect her appearance or her disposition and when it is done at this age, there is no reason why the bitch should become overweight. All the Guide Dogs for the Blind are spayed, and it is obvious that this does not affect their ability to work. However, if you have a top-quality specimen of the breed, it seems rather a waste to have her neutered, as she will never have the opportunity to

Ch. Fromestaff Nettle of Wyrefare: Males and females are equally loving and affectionate in temperament. If you choose a female you will have to cope with her seasonal cycle.

Ch. Lethal Weapon of Crashcon: The male Stafford is more powerfully built and more muscular than the female.

pass on her excellent qualities. If you have no plans to breed, it is better to choose a bitch that is slightly inferior in type, who will still make an excellent companion, rather than deprive the breed of a potentially important producer.

ASSESSING THE LITTER

When you are choosing a Stafford, you will want to know what the puppy is going to look like as an adult. This is very difficult unless you are very familiar with the breed. If this is not the case, you will have to rely on the breeder to guide you in your choice.

The most important thing to look for is that the litter is fit and healthy, and has been reared in a clean, hygienic environment. The puppies should be plump and lively, with a good coat and clear eyes. If you are looking for a puppy with show potential, you want to see a sturdy, short-backed puppy, with rose-shaped ears and round eyes. The head should be short and strong with a wide muzzle. The teeth should be set in a terrier bite, i.e. the top teeth fitting tightly over the bottom

When you are choosing a puppy, it is important to check that all the puppies are fit and healthy, and they should also be friendly and out-going.

The puppy's head should be short and strong with a wide muzzle.

At ten weeks of age, this puppy of Dumbriton breeding is showing good overall development, with excellent bone and substance.

For the pet owner, temperament is all-important: you are looking for a dog who will fit in with your lifestyle and will provide years of happy companionship.

teeth, with a good, strong underjaw. There should be a bit of length to the forelegs, which will give the chest room to develop. The front should be strong with plenty of bone and substance. The feet will usually look big and out of proportion, but this is nothing to worry about, as the puppy will quickly grow into them! Even at eight to ten weeks, the bend of stifle should be evident, and the male should have two testicles descended into the scrotum.

Good breeding is all-important, but the type of rearing you give over the crucial months of growing and development will also play an influential part in how the adult dog turns out. Do not pay so much attention to appearance that you forget personality. A fearless, bouncy, puppy will be easy to train, and an extrovert character will be an advantage when it comes to showing. A more serious, gentle puppy may well have the makings of a faithful companion.

Do not make the mistake of saying that you want a family pet, hoping you will get a show-quality puppy at a bargain price. It is essential that the breeder is aware of your requirements. It is equally important to remember that show 'faults' will not affect your Stafford's personality, nor its future health and well-being. A dog that has any of the following 'faults': overshot or undershot in the jaw, flat feet or over-sized feet, too long in the back, too short in the leg, too long or too short in the muzzle, too narrow in the skull, almond eyes, full-prick ears or a short Bulldog tail – will be penalised in the show ring, but these 'faults' will not detract from a healthy Stafford's good looks or character.

Most purchasers are anxious to buy a reasonable specimen of the breed even if they have no intentions of showing. So, the best thing to do is to explain your requirements to the breeder, and you will be shown the best puppies within your price range.

AFTER-SALES SERVICE

If you have selected a responsible, caring breeder, you should be given all the necessary paperwork when you make your purchase, plus a diet sheet, and possibly some food for the puppy's first few meals in the new home. Most breeders are only too happy to be contacted to give advice and information following the sale, and many purchasers keep in touch with the breeder for many years to come.

Remember, if you have bought a show-quality puppy, there is no guarantee that you will go on to win in the show ring. The breeder can only assess puppies for their show potential, and many things can change as the puppy grows and develops.

Chapter Six

TRAINING YOUR STAFFORD

UNDERSTANDING YOUR DOG

The first essential for anyone undertaking the training of a dog – even just house training a pet Stafford – is a thorough understanding of the dog's mind and its limitations. You must also possess the ability to appreciate what passes through the dog's mind.

A dog is primarily a creature of habit, and can be readily taught by means of the association of ideas. This fact must be clearly understood and mastered by the trainer, because if it is wrongly

Ch. Mistress McGrath of Boldmore: In order to train your Stafford, you must first understand how a dog's mind works.

It is not long before the appealing little puppy becomes a strong-willed adolescent, so it is essential to start on a programme of discipline from an early stage.

used it will create the opposite effect to that desired. The next thing to grasp is that all dogs have strong inborn instincts, the strength of which varies with individuals, as in humans, and also among family lines, chiefly as a result of selective breeding.

No one can deny that dogs have intelligence, and there can be mental deficiency in dogs as well as in people, but a dog's reasoning powers are exceedingly limited. It is not right to compare any animal's senses or feelings with those of human beings, but I consider 'dog sense', however it may be defined, as closely akin to human reasoning power, although very limited in degree. Dogs have long memories, and for this reason a lesson wrongly learned is exceedingly difficult to rectify. By the same token, a dog treated unjustly, or deceived, will never forget the injustice.

The whole principle of dog training is therefore to utilise and develop the natural senses possessed by the dog. In the first place, habit can be instilled into a dog, as we have seen in the chapter dealing with feeding and management, where the importance of regularity was stressed. Secondly, in the training of the dog, we employ the manipulation of canine instincts, reinforced by the association of ideas. There is a great pitfall in the latter concept, in that wrong use or lack of thought can introduce bad faults into the dog, which are much more difficult to eradicate than to teach a new lesson. For example, it has been pointed out that a dog's reasoning powers are very limited, and if when a dog comes home he is beaten for going off on his own, he will associate the beating with his return home, not with being away. Such a thoughtless attempt at correction on the part of an ignorant trainer will intensify the fault instead of correcting it.

DISCIPLINE

My system of dog training can be summed up in one word – discipline. In exactly the same way, a soldier is taught by constant drill to instantly obey a lawful command without questioning the whys and wherefores, instinctively carrying out the operation as he has been taught to do. A soldier can never be trained by brutality, but only by his superior officer having gained his respect and trust — and so it is with the dog. The animal's very limited reasoning powers make it easier to obtain implicit obedience, but mean it is even more important to ensure that the order is just and readily understood.

The attributes essential in a dog trainer are similar to those needed in a good officer: scrupulous fairness, absolute justness in his commands, a quiet manner, firm but gentle, without undue sloppiness, and a quiet voice. Loss of patience or temper is fatal in the training of a dog, and these usually go with a loud, shouting voice which will only bewilder a dog, as it does most men. A dog well knows if his master loses his temper, and will lose confidence in him. Injustice and deception are things which no dog can understand, and they never forgive nor forget. As with a child, it is never too early to commence simple lessons in regular habits, association of ideas and discipline, but, similarly, the lessons must be exceedingly simple and easily understood, and no attempt must be made at serious schooling until the mind is properly formed.

From the time they are first weaned, puppies can be taught regular habits by regularity in their hours of feeding, grooming, and exercise. If the puppy is put outdoors, or placed on an earth tray if more convenient, immediately after each meal, it will readily learn that this is the time and place to perform the functions of nature. This brings up a simple example of what is meant by the necessity of the trainer being able to understand the dog's mind, and to think as a dog thinks. If a dog is wandering round the room, sniffing at various places, it can be readily understood by anyone that it is looking for a place to defecate. The pup must be rapidly intercepted and taken to the correct spot. Luckily, a dog's brain works comparatively slowly and the trainer must always be on the alert to sense what the dog is contemplating, and to forestall him if it is an undesirable action. Learn to think as a dog thinks, and quicker than he does – this is the secret of successfully training your Staffordshire Bull Terrier.

BASIC PRINCIPLES

By association of ideas and example, a dog can be taught practically anything, but he must be shown exactly what is required of him, and the lesson must be repeated over and over again until thoroughly learned. This is where unlimited patience comes in. Although constant repetition is necessary, each lesson must be short, especially with puppies. When obedience is gained, that lesson should be concluded for the day. It is essential that the dog's attention is not distracted, and that he does not become tired and bored.

When the point of a lesson is grasped, the pupil should be given all the praise possible and allowed to relax. It is an old-fashioned idea that "the nearest way to a dog's heart is down his throat" but, while the occasional tidbit (not sweets or sugar) is quite in order, the principle is not a good one. Much more can be achieved by sweet-voiced praise and a little fussing and patting.

Corrections must be given with the greatest of care, and the trainer must be absolutely positive that the order was understood in the first place, so that the dog understands exactly where he has gone wrong. If the dog has not understood, he must be carefully shown again and again. For example, if the dog is being taught to sit, and remain, in an appointed place, he must be placed on that spot, the hindquarters gently depressed, the word of command given several times, and the hands gradually removed. When the dog, as he is sure to at first, gets up and moves away, he must be picked up, gently scolded, placed again on the spot, and the lesson repeated. When in the

A puppy has a limited concentration span, so lessons must be kept short, and the puppy must be rewarded with plenty of praise.

correct position again, the slightly scolding tone should be changed to one of praise. The old adage "A Spaniel, a woman and a walnut tree, the more you whip them the better they be" is not true as far as the dog is concerned, and chastisement should be avoided if at all possible. In only one case is it really necessary, and that is for rank, premeditated, and thoroughly understood disobedience. If the punishment is well done, it need never be repeated, but it is essential that the dog clearly understands what it is for. It should be given at the time and place of the offence and administered on the correct part of the body, which is the same as that for small boys, in other words, the rear end. When training a dog, an order must never be given unless the trainer is in a position to compel the animal to obey.

VOCABULARY AND VOICE
For the proper control of your Stafford, especially at a distance, a vocabulary of words of command is necessary, and this should be as short and as simple as possible. Dogs do not understand our language, or any other, in spite of what some sentimental owners like to think, but they do recognise the different sounds and tones of voice. "Music soothes the savage beast" is a truism, and dogs certainly enjoy being talked to in a quiet, nicely-modulated voice. The chosen words of command should be short, clear, and as different from each other as possible.

EARLY LESSONS
The first lesson a puppy must be taught is cleanliness. As already mentioned, this training can be commenced as soon as the puppies are weaned, and with gentle care and regularity should be easily and rapidly accomplished. Care must be taken to give the pup ample opportunity to use the correct place at frequent intervals, especially after a meal. If this is done and, in addition, careful

Austrian Ch. Cheersytaff's Brindle Abigail: When you progress to controlling your Stafford at a distance, make sure you keep your commands short and simple.

observation kept in order to anticipate and prevent the action, "mistakes" will be rare. If an accident should occur, the culprit should be taken to the spot, shown the mess, gently scolded and immediately put outside or on to the earth tray. Beating a tiny puppy is brutal and entirely unnecessary, and the old-fashioned custom of "rubbing his nose in it" is a filthy waste of time, which has nothing to recommend it.

In a similar manner, a dog can easily be trained not to climb on chairs or other places which are not allowed, and taught when indoors to sit quietly on the hearthrug or in his own box. Stealing food is also simple to prevent. If the dog is fed regularly, always on the same spot and in his own bowl, and is never given tidbits at the table during meals, he will soon learn to regard human meals and food as no concern of his.

Gentle play with the puppy in the garden will gradually encourage him to learn his own name, and to come to his owner when called. No serious training must be attempted until the pup is four or five months old, and it is a great mistake to attempt to take puppies for walks, other than in the garden, before they are strong enough. A thin, light collar can be put on the puppy for a few minutes each day, care being taken to see that the collar does not irritate and cause the puppy to scratch. The periods of wear of the collar can be gradually lengthened until the dog has it on all day. It is preferable to remove the collar when the dog is finally put to bed at night and to replace it, after cleaning it and grooming the dog, first thing in the morning.

LEAD TRAINING

When the puppy has become used to his collar, and grown and gained in strength enough to be taken for very short walks, training on the lead can begin. At first, your pup will run round and round in circles and get tangled up between your legs, but with patience and gradual shortening of the lead, he can be accustomed to the correct position. This is close in to the handler's left leg, with the dog's nose in line with the handler's left knee, the lead being held in the left hand, fairly loose, but not sufficiently long to get tangled round lamp-posts or the legs of passers-by.

The correct leading position having been taught at the halt (the lessons for this should be of short duration and extremely well taught), the handler can take a pace forward and at the same time give a simple word of command such as "Come". The dog is sure to hang back at first, and must be gently coaxed forward by manipulation of the lead, the word of command being repeated at the same time. Gradually the pup will learn to walk on the lead, but will be all over the place at first. He must be gradually taught to walk along properly close in to, and in line with, the handler's left leg. This can be gradually accomplished by frequent short lessons, the dog being kept in position by a gentle pull forward or backward to the correct place, with the repetition of the commands "Come" and "Heel".

A dog which continually surges forward to the extent of the lead can be cured by the handler carrying a rolled-up newspaper, for tapping the dog's nose when he gets in front of the handler's left leg, at the same time repeating the command "Heel". Nothing looks worse than to see a dog at the extreme extent of its lead — taking its owner for a walk — to say nothing of the nuisance to other pedestrians. On the other hand, nothing looks better than to see a perfectly-trained dog, following close to heel on a loose lead, and stopping and standing quietly when his owner stops.

Never hit your dog with its collar or lead, as this will make it nervous of having them put on. In fact, never hit a dog with your hand, or with anything else when it comes to you after being called, and never snatch at the dog when it does so. Such behaviour will make him circle round when he comes to your call, and he will be nervous of coming within reach of the hand.

The dog should be taught to stand at heel whenever the handler halts, and to remain standing as long as he is stationary. In this way, the dog will not be a nuisance to passers-by if the owner stops to speak to an acquaintance, and will not be a constant source of anxiety regarding his whereabouts. This having been taught, it is comparatively simple to train a dog to remain standing on command for considerable periods.

SUMMARY

The whole principle of dog training is patience and constant demonstration on the above lines, and with them, a dog can be taught almost anything. To sum up, remember that dogs are creatures of habit, they love regularity and easily learn by imitation and demonstration. Make all lessons simple and of short duration, especially in the early stages, and consisting of one thing only. When the pupil has once grasped the thing being taught, discontinue the lesson for that day. Do not overtax the dog's brain, and allow frequent intervals for relaxation and play. Be firm but gentle, and make quite sure that the dog understands what is being taught. Use simple, clear words of command. Be certain the dog knows what he did wrong before punishing him, and always give the punishment at the exact spot the disobedience occurred. Never give an order unless it is possible to enforce obedience.

Chapter Seven

CARING FOR YOUR STAFFORD

GENERAL MANAGEMENT OF DOGS

In order to live and be healthy, an animal requires food, water and exercise. In addition to these, a domesticated animal which is to a great extent dependent on man, requires accommodation and some assistance towards cleanliness. Moreover, domesticated animals become creatures of habit and regularity, much more so than they would in the wild.

In dog management, regularity is of the utmost importance. All Stafford owners must be prepared to sacrifice something, and to give up a certain amount of time to the well-being of their pet. Routine can be arranged to the convenience of the owner, but the times of feeding, grooming, exercise and letting out for the purposes of nature, should be as fixed and regular as possible.

Jolaine Sir Dan: The Stafford is an easy dog to care for, as long as you adopt a regime of providing good-quality food, daily exercise, and regular grooming.

Practically all Staffords, both those kept in kennels or in the house, are clean by nature and suffer a great deal from not being allowed outside to relieve themselves. Your Stafford should always be allowed out of doors for a few minutes first thing in the morning, shortly after food, last thing at night, and at frequent intervals throughout the day.

A full-grown, healthy Stafford requires only one good meal per day, and this may be given at whatever time is best suited to the owner, as long as this is approximately the same time each day. In the case of a house pet, you will probably find it most convenient to feed after the family's midday meal, but for a larger number of kennel dogs, the ideal time is about 4pm. This meal can be gradually delayed as the evenings draw out, so it can be an hour later at the height of summer.

Although one meal a day is sufficient for a Stafford, a small snack may be given first thing in the morning, just something to break the dog's fast, such as a large biscuit. Water should be accessible to the dog at all times. A good clean, strong dish should be placed where the Stafford can easily reach it, yet where it cannot be knocked over. A stainless steel bowl is best in both house and kennel. The water must be constantly changed, especially in hot and dusty weather.

KENNELLING

Why should we need to kennel our dogs? In normal circumstances, Staffordshire Bull Terriers are kept as pets, and most people are quite happy just to let them have the run of the house. I have found that if you are serious showgoers, and own more than one dog, it is more beneficial for you and the dogs if they are kennelled. The most important reason for this is – and I hate to say it – fighting. If you leave three or four Staffordshire Bull Terriers together you are asking for trouble.

A couple of Staffords will usually live together in harmony, but if you plan to keep a larger number of dogs, you will need to kennel them.

The little games they play could soon become the real thing. When that glazed look comes over their eyes and their lips go back, you can soon have a crisis on your hands and possibly one or even two dead dogs. Hence the reason to kennel them.

But let's start with the one-dog owner. You have to decide right at the very beginning whether you want to kennel your Stafford or not. Let me say this before we go any further. We have found that a dog kept out in the fresh air is always healthier than one kept indoors, but we must also say that if you have bought the dog for protection, it won't be much use if the dog is outside in a kennel while your house is being robbed. If you decide on a kennel, it is obviously an advantage to have it within easy access of the house. Your Stafford is then near enough to detect strange sounds and movements about the premises and can give the alarm promptly, but it is also more convenient when you are carrying out food in wet or stormy weather, or attending to your dog in the event of illness.

KENNEL DIMENSIONS
The kennel should be on high ground, preferably facing south, for the sake of sunlight and protection from north and east winds. It should have a run attached, no less than 6ft x 5ft, which provides enough room for play and exercise. The frontage of the kennel should preferably face and be within view of the house windows. Your particular situation, however, will be determined by circumstances and the amount of ground space available. No owner these days should put a valuable dog to live and sleep in an old-fashioned makeshift 'Fido' kennel, to which the animal was attached by a short chain. It is generally accepted that the most suitable shelter is one in which the dog has plenty of room in which to lie crosswise, to stand upright, and turn round to stretch himself. The main requirements are ample space for unrestrained movement, a comfortable sleeping bench, well raised from the ground and protected from damp and draughts, plenty of light, adequate air-vents and scrupulous cleanliness.

Warmth is a minor consideration. A healthy dog, properly fed and exercised, will not suffer from cold if its bedding is sufficient and dry. A cold atmosphere is more suitable for the canine constitution, and certainly better for the growth of a shining coat, than the artificial warmth provided by a fire or central heating. Many dog owners like to design and build their own kennels, in the belief that this is a more economical method than buying one ready-made. Take it from me, it is far cheaper to buy a ready-made kennel from one of the better known established firms. Purpose-built kennels are planned on scientific, sanitary principles, and constructed in portable sections which can be assembled and erected in any suitable location. They may also include many appliances which may be overlooked by the individual attempting to build a kennel with his own materials.

THE KENNEL RANGE
In an extensive breeding establishment, and by that I mean more than four animals, it becomes necessary to have a range of kennels. It is cheaper if these are all together with several compartments partitioned off under one roof, each having its own door and run attached. At certain times of year, when your bitches come into season, you will have to house them in a separate kennel. This kennel should be well away from the unit for isolation purposes. It can also double as a whelping kennel and as a spare in case of illness. If there is plenty of room, there is no objection to two friendly dogs occupying the same cubicle, but no more. Two is company, three's a crowd, and that's asking for trouble.

In fact, it is better if each dog has his own kennel. In this way, fights will never start. However many separate kennels there may be, and however they are distributed, the difference is in numbers only. Each kennel by itself should be strong and secure against escape, as well as weatherproof and, most importantly, free from draughts and lingering dampness. Never keep hens where you have dogs, because they encourage rats, who will search out every bit of food that the dogs leave. Rats also mean fleas and infection, and they will waste no time in making burrows under the floor. These little devils will even eat through two inches of concrete. When I put the bottoming in under the concrete, I lace it with pieces of glass, at which the rats, when they come across it, back off and will not try to burrow there again.

Ventilation is achieved by open gratings above the door, and airholes under the eaves, as well as a window which can be opened, by pushing it out from the bottom. The window should have two catches on either side of it, as a safety measure.

EQUIPMENT

A bench or portable sleeping box, big enough to enable the dog to lie at full stretch in any position, should be raised several inches above the floor. Bedding should be a heavy blanket, which should be changed whenever necessary. You should also disinfect the kennel every day, and give it a good scrub-out once a week. Rejected food, old bones, crumbs or biscuits should also be swept out every day. The fewer things left lying about in the kennel the better. A drinking dish alone is necessary, and this should be regularly and frequently replenished with clean water.

Every dog kennel should have a good water supply, with a standard tap for adjusting the necessary hose and flushing the runs. All refuse, such as old bones, rejected food, excreta, paper

Ch. Pitbar Rebel Warlord: In order to keep in peak condition, a Stafford requires a programme of daily outdoor exercise.

Raymond.

and so forth, should be promptly burned and, for this purpose, an incinerator is a great advantage.

Where only one or two dogs are kept, a more modest plan must be adopted in a single or double self-contained portable kennel, with its own railed-in run. There are many such kennels supplied by discerning manufacturers, furnished with every convenience, strong, weatherproof, comfortable and inexpensive. Such a kennel should be erected near your house for greater facility of feeding, cleaning and general management. One advantage of a portable kennel is the obvious one — it can easily be taken to pieces and re-erected on a new site if desired.

EXERCISE

A Stafford requires vigorous outdoor exercise daily. It is impossible to lay down hard and fast rules regarding the amount of exercise necessary, but take as a rough guide that a Stafford needs a good hour's scramble in the country, covering at least twice the distance his master does. Double this time if the dog is exercised on the lead in the streets.

The Stafford should be taken for exercise at approximately the same time each day, the best time being before his food. Early afternoon (except in the height of summer) is usually the best part of the day. This is another reason why it is best to feed kennel dogs in the late afternoon. Walks can give the greatest enjoyment to both the owner and Stafford, provided there is a sympathetic understanding between the two, and an intelligent 'conversation' is carried on between them. No Stafford will take sufficient exercise on his own, however large the garden or run in which he is let out.

Ch. Rocellio Rip Van Winkle: The short-coated Stafford needs little more than a regular brush and massage. Grooming sessions should also be used as a way of keeping a daily check on your dog's general condition.

GROOMING

A Stafford requires regular grooming, not only to cleanse the coat, but to stimulate the muscles and the growth of the hair, and also to remove dead hairs. Many Staffords dislike being groomed, and are afraid of a brush. This happens because of rough handling and being hit with the back of the brush. With proper handling – talking to and making much of the dog – the process of grooming can be a joy for both owner and pet.

Stand your Stafford on a table at about waist height to avoid backache for the handler. With a good hound glove (one with little rubber nodules on it), start at the head and continue over the whole body, brushing vigorously against the lie of the coat in long sweeping movements. Put as much weight as possible behind the brush, and continue for as long as possible. This is the massage which tones up the system and does so much good. As your Stafford has a smooth coat, a finish off with a chamois leather will give a fine gloss to it.

When it comes to bath time – and this should not be too often as it destroys the natural oil in the coat – you should use a shower spray with lukewarm water, and a good brand of special dog shampoo or baby shampoo. At no time should carbolic soap or washing-up liquid be used. The dog should be thoroughly rinsed, then immediately dried and briskly towelled down.

DAILY CHECKS

The grooming period should also be utilised to give your Stafford his daily inspection. Starting at the head, see that the eyes are bright and clean, and the nose cool and damp, with no sign of discharge. The ears should be dry and clean, and free from any offensive smell. Gums should be firm and pink, teeth clean and free from fur, and the breath without smell. The whole of the coat must be examined to ensure that it is free from fleas or other parasites. Favourite harbouring places are the roots of the ears, the armpits and the root of the tail, so these areas need special attention. The skin should be carefully examined to make sure there are no red blotches or eruptions.

Careful inspection should be made of the feet to see that there are no cysts forming between the toes, and that the pads are not too hard and cracked, or too soft and sore. A careful check should be made to ensure that the nails do not become too long. The dewclaws should receive special care, as these nails have no contact with the ground and can easily grow right round and pierce the pad.

There should be no discharge from the anus or the genital organs, and a constant watch should be kept on bitches for signs of their coming in season. The general condition of your Stafford should be noted, to see that the skin is loose from the body, the stomach not distended, and that the dog is his normal lively self. 'Condition' is a difficult thing to explain, but a good stockman – who is born, not made — can tell at a glance if his charges are in good condition or not. This instinct is a question of experience, and of individually knowing each animal under your charge.

FEEDING REGIME

The necessity of regularity in feeding has already been stressed, so now let us consider the foods essential to a dog's well-being. It must be remembered that the dog is by nature carnivorous and needs a fair proportion of flesh in his diet. A dog's teeth are designed to tear up his prey, and chew off large chunks of flesh with a proportion of skin, hair and bones. The dog's stomach is designed to bolt a fairly large meal at one time, and his gastric juices are so strong that they can even dissolve bones, although this is a fairly slow process.

Your Stafford therefore requires a pretty large meal at one time, and one good meal a day is sufficient for a grown dog. Time must be given afterwards for its proper digestion. The meal must consist of meat and some form of roughage, to take the place of hide and hair and to assist digestion. For the meat there is nothing as good as fresh lean beef, mutton or breast of lamb. All are excellent for putting on weight. Ox-heart or cheek, liver and tripe are all wholesome, natural foods that your Stafford will relish from time to time. You can get most of these foods in your local pet shop, in either 1lb or 2lb frozen packs. You put the contents into warm water and scald for five minutes.

I am not a great believer in complete foods, as there are so many excellent alternatives to them. Petfood manufacturers have perfected an enormous range of tinned foods and biscuits, either for puppies or mature dogs. Fish has very good food value and is a useful alternative. Various types of fish, especially the flesh of a kipper, will often tempt a sick dog who refuses other food. Milk is also good for your dog, and the best type of all is goat's milk, especially recommended for puppies and bitches in whelp.

ROUGHAGE

To supply roughage, and also to provide a certain amount of nourishment, some form of biscuit meal should be given. Every endeavour should be made to obtain biscuit made by a reputable manufacturer. Biscuit meal made from pure wholemeal wheat flour is the best, and if you can afford to feed wholemeal bread, the nourishment value is excellent. Ordinary brown bread is also good, but never feed white bread. Table scraps can be fed to your dog, and they make a good change from his normal diet. Scraps of cooked meat or gristle are fine, but any highly seasoned food must be avoided. Salt is certainly bad for your dog, as are all forms of sweet foods, which should be avoided because of the effect on teeth and digestion. In some cases, sugar can also cause skin problems.

A dog's food should on no account be sloppy, as this weakens the digestive system and causes gastric and skin trouble. The majority of such illnesses can be traced to faulty feeding. Biscuit meal is manufactured in various sizes, the terrier type being the most suitable for Staffords. Such meal may be fed dry. The ideal thing to do with the biscuit is to cover it with boiling water, leave it to soak for an hour or so with the bowl covered, and then thoroughly squeeze it out. The resultant crumbling, dry meal should be mixed with good fresh, raw meat, cut in pieces about the size of Oxo cubes, then fed to your dog.

Another treat I give my dogs is a stockpot of vegetables and a big beef bone. This makes an excellent soup which is then poured over some biscuits and allowed to soak in well. Again, take care that it does not become sloppy. The temperature of all meals should be quite cool, as very hot food will be certain to upset the digestion. In feeding our modern dog, we have deprived his teeth of their natural function of tearing up prey and grinding the bones, and, unless we provide an alternative, they will soon decay or develop other troubles. There is nothing finer for this purpose than a fresh, clean marrow bone – the larger the better. If you keep more than one dog, you must separate them unless you want a real 'donnybrook' on your hands. I have known dogs who have lived together all their lives try to tear each other apart over a bone. Remember that you own a Stafford, whose fighting potential lies just under the skin. Give him a bone or large biscuit twice a week. It will do his teeth the world of good, and is a useful way of preventing him getting bored.

Chapter Eight

THE BREED STANDARD

The Stafford, whose history we have traced, was first registered with the UK Kennel Club in 1935, and the modern Standard, published in 1987, is reproduced below. This Standard was also approved by the FCI (the European governing body) countries in June, 1987.

THE BRITISH BREED STANDARD

GENERAL APPEARANCE
Smooth-coated, well-balanced, of great strength for his size. Muscular, active and agile.

CHARACTERISTICS
Traditionally of indomitable courage and tenacity. Highly intelligent, especially with children.

TEMPERAMENT
Bold, fearless and totally reliable.

HEAD AND SKULL
Short, deep through with broad skull. Very pronounced cheek muscles, distinct stop, short foreface, nose black.

EYES
Dark preferred, but may bear some relation to coat colour. Round, of medium size and set to look straight ahead. Eye rims dark.

EARS
Rose or half pricked, not large or heavy. Full drop or pricked ears highly undesirable.

MOUTH
Lips tight and clean. Jaws strong, teeth large, with a perfect, regular and complete scissor bite, i.e. upper teeth closely overlapping the lower teeth and set square to the jaws.

NECK
Muscular, rather short, clean in outline, gradually widening towards the shoulders.

POINTS OF ANATOMY
As illustrated by Ch. Eastaff Guardian

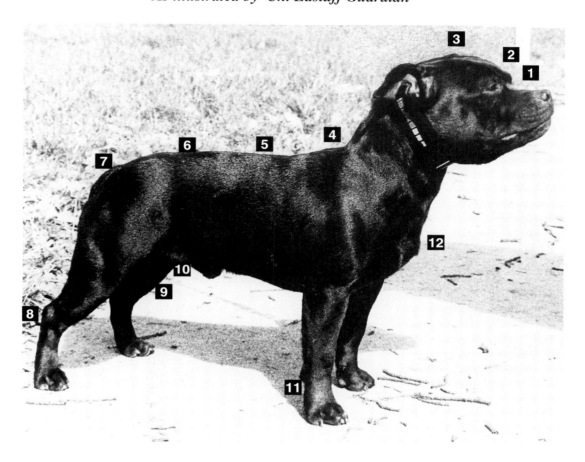

Key

1. Muzzle	5. Back	9. Stifle
2. Stop	6. Loin	10. Tuck up
3. Occiput	7. Croup	11. Pastern
4. Withers	8 Hock	12. Forechest.

FOREQUARTERS
Legs straight and well boned, set rather wide apart, showing no weakness at the pasterns, from which point feet turn out a little. Shoulders well laid back, with no looseness at elbow.

BODY
Close coupled, with level topline, wide front, deep brisket, well sprung ribs, muscular and well defined.

HINDQUARTERS
Well muscled, hocks well let down with stifles well bent. Legs parallel when viewed from behind.

FEET
Well padded, strong and of medium size. Nails black in solid coloured dogs.

TAIL
Medium length, low set, tapering to a point and carried rather low. Should not curl much, and may be likened to an old-fashioned pump handle.

GAIT AND MOVEMENT
Free, powerful and agile, with economy of effort, legs moving parallel when viewed from front or rear. Discernible drive from hind legs.

COAT
Smooth, short and close.

COLOUR
Red, fawn, white, black or blue, or any one of these colours with white. Any shade of brindle or any shade of brindle with white. Black and tan, or liver colour highly undesirable.

SIZE
Weight: Dogs – 28 to 38 lbs. Bitches – 24 to 34 lbs. Desirable height (at withers) 14 to 16 inches, these heights being related to the weights.

FAULTS
Any departure from the foregoing points should be considered a fault, and the seriousness with which the fault should be regarded should be in exact proportion to the degree.

Reproduced by kind permission of the English Kennel Club.

THE AMERICAN BREED STANDARD

GENERAL APPEARANCE
The Staffordshire Bull Terrier is a smooth-coated dog. It should be of great strength for its size and, although muscular, should be active and agile.

SIZE, PROPORTION, SUBSTANCE
Height at shoulder: 14 to 16 inches. Weight: Dogs, 28 to 38 pounds; bitches 24 to 34 pounds, these heights being related to the weights. Non-conformity with these limits is a fault. In proportion, the length of back from withers to tailset, is equal to the distance from withers to ground.

HEAD
Short, deep through, broad skull, very pronounced cheek muscles, distinct stop, short foreface, black nose. Pink (Dudley) nose to be considered a serious fault. *Eyes* – Dark preferable, but may bear some relation to coat color. Round, of medium size, and set to look straight ahead. Light eyes or pink eye rims to be considered a fault, except that where the coat surrounding the eye is white the eye rim may be pink. *Ears* – Rose or half-pricked and not large. Full drop or full prick to be considered a serious fault. *Mouth* – A bite in which the outer side of the lower incisors touches the inner side of the upper incisors. The lips should be tight, and clean. The badly undershot or overshot bite is a serious fault.

NECK, TOPLINE, BODY
The neck is muscular, rather short clean in outline and gradually widening toward the shoulders. The body is close coupled, with a level topline, wide front, deep brisket and well sprung ribs being rather light in the loins. The tail is undocked, of medium length, low set, tapering to a point and carried rather low. It should not curl much and may be likened to an old-fashioned pump handle. A tail that is too long or badly curled is a fault.

FOREQUARTERS
Legs straight and well boned, set rather far apart, without looseness at the shoulders and showing no weakness at the pasterns, from which point the feet turn out a little. Dewclaws on the forelegs may be removed. The feet should be well padded, strong and of medium size.

HINDQUARTERS
The hindquarters should be well muscled, hocks let down with stifles well bent. Legs should be parallel when viewed from behind. Dewclaws if any, on the hind legs are generally removed. Feet as in front.

COAT
Smooth, short and close to the skin, not to be trimmed or de-whiskered.

COLOR
Red, fawn, white, black or blue, or any of these colors with white. Any shade of brindle or any shade of brindle with white. Black-and-tan or liver colour to be disqualified.

GAIT
Free, powerful and agile with economy of effort. Legs moving parallel when viewed from front or rear. Discernible drive from hind legs.

TEMPERAMENT
From the past history of the Staffordshire Bull Terrier, the modern dog draws its character of indomitable courage, high intelligence, and tenacity. This, coupled with its affection for its

friends and children in particular, its off-duty quietness and trustworthy stability, makes it a foremost all-purpose dog.

DISQUALIFICATION
Black-and-tan or liver color.

Approved November, 14, 1989.
Reproduced by kind permission of the American Kennel Club.

INTERPRETATION OF THE STANDARD

All individuals interpret the standard as they see it, and all the Kennel Club does is to direct them as to what is laid down. You will never get two enthusiasts agreeing on all points of the standard. People who are faddists and go for the extreme type will always try to shape the direction of the breed by putting up friends with the same type of dog as they keep themselves, and through this practice, fads develop. Ringsiders at shows see this, and before you know where you are, they use the preferred stud dogs whose extremes are thus perpetuated in the breed.

The more enlightened breeder should be guided along a path which aims for perfection in the Staffordshire Bull Terrier. As I have said, no two people see the standard with the same mind's eye view. On the other hand, it is most important that they not only 'understand' it, but that they can apply it when they look at specimens they intend to use at stud, and also, of course, the dogs they judge. It is also crucial to discuss with knowledgeable competitors, who are not faddists and whose integrity is beyond reproach, the potential use of one or two very good stud dogs. By doing this the 'standard' type of Staffordshire Bull Terrier will soon be not only implanted in their minds, but there for all to see.

GENERAL APPEARANCE
A good Staffordshire Bull Terrier should possess the most important thing in any breed, and that is 'type'. This word 'type' is like a piece of elastic — it stretches the whole way round the dog. He must possess the basic attributes of well-formed physical features. But to be really good, the Staffordshire Bull Terrier must also possess what some people would call 'quality'. If an individual dog has this, it will stick out like a sore thumb, while the animal without that 'Q' factor will be just as obvious by the failings in its appearance.

Expression is very important too. That quizzical look on the face — no wonder the Stafford was called the "laughing dog" – will be missing if the eyes are wrongly set in the head. This will also happen if they are too large or too small, or if the colour is wrong. Years ago a very prominent Stafford judge told me that light eyes were perfectly alright, because the dog could see better in the dark. Well, did you ever – I think he must have been thinking of a cat! An eye that is too light in colour spoils the dog's expression, so the darker they are, the better. The only time you should accept a lighter eye should be in relation to the coat colour; but let me reiterate: do not accept too light an eye, no matter what colour the coat is.

Although the Staffordshire Bull Terrier is, to my mind, a 'pocket battleship', elegance is very important, and this comes only from correct balance and soundness, good, well-shaped bone and proper distribution of the muscle, which gives that athletic look so important to this breed. The Stafford's conformation must have complete co-ordination of body and limbs, to give that beautiful, natural, flowing action, no matter which angle he is viewed from. All his parts, i.e. head,

Ch. Black Ice: The Stafford should look like a 'pocket battleship', showing an elegance that comes from correct balance and soundness.

Dalton.

Ch. Boldbull Blackjack: The Stafford is sometimes known as the 'laughing dog' because of the breed's typical expression.

Raymond.

EYES

Correct: Round-shaped, medium-sized.

Incorrect: Too large.

Incorrect: Almond-shaped.

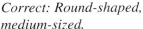

neck, shoulders, body, hindquarters, should flow into each other to produce a dog that is ultra-sound and a joy to behold on the move. There should be a free, powerful and agile movement, with economy of effort, legs moving parallel when viewed from front or rear, and a discernible drive from the hindlegs.

HEAD AND SKULL

The head should be short, with a deep through broad skull, very pronounced cheek muscles, a distinct stop, a short foreface, and a black nose. The Staffordshire Bull Terrier is like lots of other breeds in that the head is classed as probably the most important part of its make-up. In other words it is a 'head breed'. The head should have a rugged beauty, with a strong, broad, short

HEAD AND SKULL

Correct: Staffordshire Bull Terrier type. The ideal head.

Terrier type head.

Bulldog type head.

muzzle with innate strength and power. This constituted the Stafford's 'tools of war', with muscles joining all round the head, to give the breed its renowned biting power. The story of the dog being able to lock his jaw is just an old wives' tale. It is tenacity and determination that make him hold on. Most Stafford breeders and judges work on a 2:1 ratio as the ideal proportion of balance for skull and muzzle. Nostrils should be big and black.

The head of a Stafford bitch should be feminine, i.e. the head should not look 'doggy' when you first look at her. The bitch who carries a 'doggy head' will always pass this on to her female offspring, who will, all things being equal, always stand second to the bitch with a more feminine head. The Stafford's head should be well 'filled up' under the eye, i.e. the surface below the eye should be filled in, which is what gives the muzzle that deep, strong look. The underjaw, when viewed from the front, should be wide and strong, not shallow or receding. It should not be snipy, and there should be no sign of a 'dishface' or a 'downface'. All these three types must be classed as very undesirable.

EARS

The ears of a Staffordshire Bull Terrier are very important to the overall appearance. If the ears are too large, are 'flying', or are too high-set, they can be a big disadvantage. The ideal ear should be small, thin and neat and most importantly, rose-shaped. The dog should be able to fold them back out in an 'aggro'. Ears of this make and shape do so much to accentuate the head and skull, a very desirable feature of the Stafford. The other type of acceptable ear placement is half-pricked, which is not so bad provided they are small, but heavier ears give the dog a 'Dumbo' effect, and ruin the

EARS

Correct: Rose-shaped ear. The ear should be small, thin and neatly-made. The fold should expose part of the inner ear. A good 'rose ear' accentuates the typical Staffordshire expression.

Half-pricked ear: acceptable.

Incorrect: Full drop ear, also known as a 'button ear'. This is highly undesirable as the ear, which is usually heavy and large, falls down the side of the head and gives a 'hound' look.

Incorrect: Erect ear. The full pricked ear is highly undesirable. It is usually caused by an extra layer of cartilage where the ear joins the skull.

whole expression. In the days of the pits, most Staffords had their ears cropped. Thank goodness that barbaric act is now a criminal offence. Full-pricked ears make the dog look like a bat. I can only remember one winner with this type of ear, a bitch called Ch. Ellasteve Bella, who was campaigned quite extensively in the 1970s before she won her title.

MOUTH

This is probably the most controversial subject in the breed, and many a debate has gone on into the wee small hours over the rights and wrongs of a Stafford's mouth. The Standard says that the mouth should be level (that is, the incisors of the lower jaw should fit closely inside the incisors of the top jaw), the teeth should be big and the lips should be tight and clean. The badly undershot or overshot mouth should be heavily penalised. If the muzzle is ultra-short, there is more chance of the animal being undershot at a later date as the underjaw gets stronger. This ultra-short muzzle also usually has the unfortunate habit of producing small teeth. We are fortunate that this type of muzzle is very rarely seen these days, due to a careful breeding programme that has seen the demise of the heavy bulldog type of head synonymous with the ultra-short muzzle.

MOUTH

Correct: Terrier bite.

Incorrect: Overshot bite.

Incorrect: undershot bite.

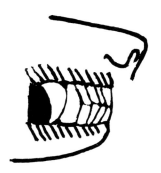

Incorrect: Level bite.

FOREQUARTERS

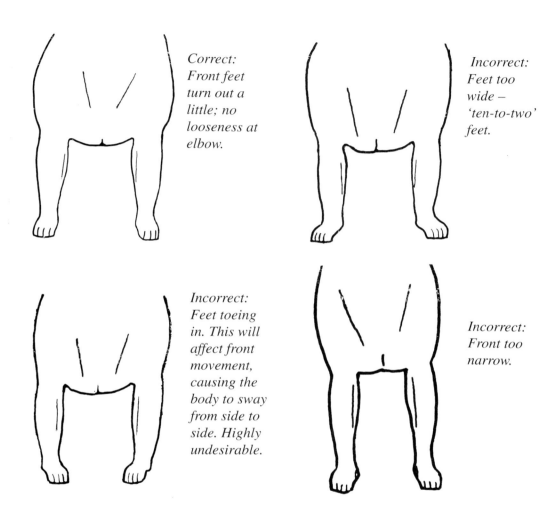

Correct: Front feet turn out a little; no looseness at elbow.

Incorrect: Feet too wide – 'ten-to-two' feet.

Incorrect: Feet toeing in. This will affect front movement, causing the body to sway from side to side. Highly undesirable.

Incorrect: Front too narrow.

FOREQUARTERS

The forelegs should be straight and well boned, set rather wide apart. This does not mean they should have a Bulldog front, but the legs should come directly underneath the dog, and the bones should be strong and firm with no bend in them. There should be no weakness at the pastern because, originally, a dog who was weak in the pastern was usually weak in his foot as well, and could not propel himself across the pit. His feet should turn out a little. His shoulders should be well laid back, which means the shoulder blades should be at a 45 degree angle, not upright. Some people think an ultra-short neck is what judges are looking for, but the ultra-short neck does not lend itself to the production of good shoulders.

Shoulder construction does influence the set-on of the neck, so the fusion between the neckline and withers should be a continuous unbroken line into the topline. The neck should not look as if it is 'stuck on', since dogs with necks like this will fail in their shoulder formation. The neck should flow smoothly into the body and be slightly arched. If a dog has a well-laid shoulder, you will find that his front movement is correct, having ample stride and easy rhythm. Upright shoulders produce a short, mincing movement like that of a Fox Terrier. The Staffordshire Bull Terrier is noted for his athletic ability and to have movement like a Fox Terrier would be disastrous.

BODY

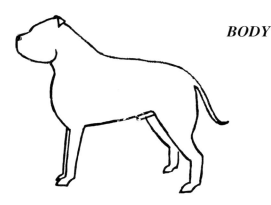

Staffordshire Bull Terrier Type
The ideal type, a good blend of 'Bull Terrier' with short, strong head, powerful short neck, good shoulders, good deep front, first class legs and feet, short back, strong hindquarters and good tail carriage.

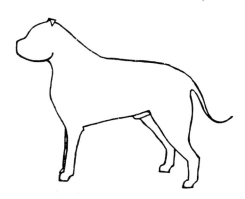

Staffordshire Bull Terrier 1940s Type
The type that did all the winning in the 1940s: lighter in bone, longer in leg and showing a bit more rib. Some judges still advocate this as the ideal.

Bulldog Type
This dog has a very short head and short neck, typical of the 'Bulldog type' with the long back that dips in the middle. Too deep in the chest, short legs, too much bone and substance.

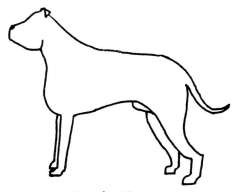

Terrier Type
The 'Terrier type': Narrow head, shallow chest, light in bone, too narrow in front with light feet. Normally good movers, being well put together. They have short backs but are too long in the neck.

BODY

The Stafford's body starts from the rib-cage on to his loin. His chest should be deep, and elbows should be well laid into his sides and tucked in. A dog in good condition physically will show this more than a dog who is lacking in development or adequate exercise. This can usually be seen in some judges' reports when they say "Needs to tighten up". They mean that the dog will improve with age or with more exercise. Judges call for a well-sprung rib-cage which has great depth, and a good level topline. We in the breed like a slight muscular arch over the loin, but deplore the roach back, which we consider a very serious and transmittable fault in any breeding programme. It is quite easy to see, as this arching of the spine over the loins is very noticeable. There should be no dip behind the withers. The Stafford is a powerful, compact dog and should have a strong back. There should be no drop in the middle of the back, nor should the back slope away at the croup. The dog should be light in his loin, his coupling should be short between his last rib and his hip joint.

HINDQUARTERS

The Staffordshire Bull Terrier has strong well-muscled hindquarters, with well let down hocks, and well bent stifles. When viewed from behind, the legs should be parallel. Well angulated and powerful hindquarters are very important to the Stafford. Only with this combination can the Stafford have the dynamic thrust it is renowned for.

Without this propulsion, the fighting dog would not have been able to move so quickly across the pit. He needed strength in his hindquarters to push against his opponent, since by being first in, he was able to get a better hold. Without those well-toned long muscles the Stafford would never have been able to do his job.

HINDQUARTERS

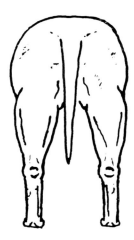

Correct.

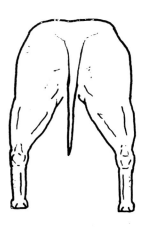

Incorrect:
Too wide.

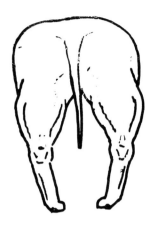

*Incorrect:
Toeing in.*

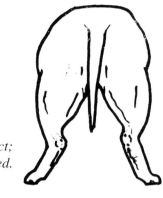

*Incorrect;
Cow-hocked.*

FEET
The feet should be strong, well-padded and of medium size. The Stafford should not have a high-knuckled foot like a cat. It should be tight and turn slightly out at the pastern. This feature was a very important part of the dog's propulsion, and can be likened to a top-class sprinter, whose feet, if you watch in slow motion, go from side to side as he comes out of the blocks. Not that the sprinter has feet that turn out at the pasterns — far from it — but he knows from experience that this action propels him forward quicker and, at the same time, pushes him into an upright position.

FEET

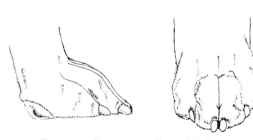

*Correct: Strong, well-padded,
of medium size*

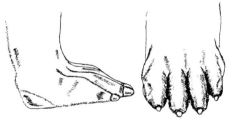

*Incorrect: Flat foot, which usually
goes with weak pasterns. The toes
are always splayed.*

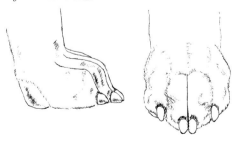

*Incorrect:
Cat foot.
Too high
on knuckle.*

The old-timers with fighting dogs were able to breed this action into their animal, knowing he had only a short distance to travel across the pit. This may seem all very scientific for those days, but it was a dire necessity, a case of winning or losing, and every little advantage counted. The ideal foot should be like a half-hare, the toes having plenty of space between them and the knuckle slightly prominent. The foot should not be splayed or flat. These sort of feet are a bad fault, as they will affect the dog's movement quite drastically, and a dog with feet like these would have been no good in the pit.

TAIL

Medium length, low set, tapering to a point and carried rather low, the tail should not curl much and may be likened to an old-fashioned pump-handle. The Stafford's tail is like a rudder, which keeps him on an even keel when he is fighting. He will move it from side to side all the time he is in a fight. The root of his tail should be strong and the tail should taper to a point. It should not be carried gaily or curl over his back and should reach to the point of the hock. If the tail is too short, it detracts from his balance. Some say that old-timers did not like a long tail because the dog who had one was usually a coward. The Stafford with a screw tail is usually far too 'bull-like' in make-up. One that comes to mind is a bitch called Ch. Spotty Lady, who was owned by Charlie Whiteworth in the early seventies.

TAIL

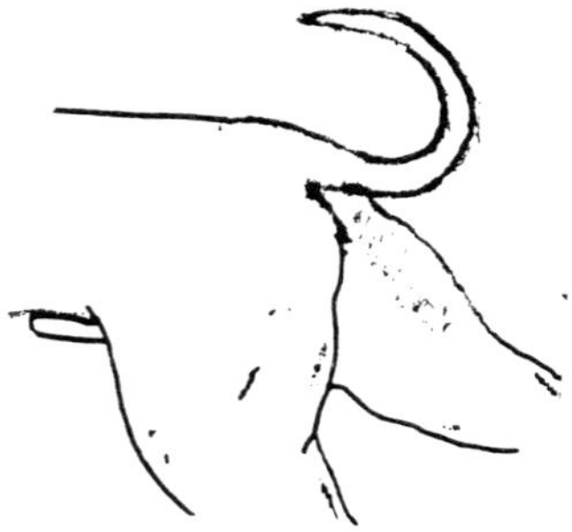

Incorrect: Tail carried too high over back.

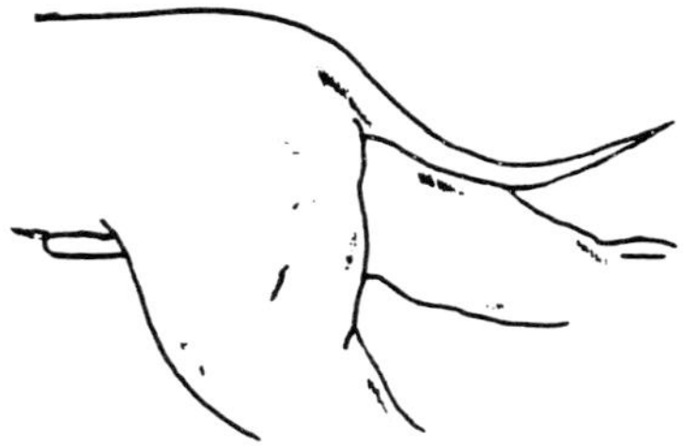

Correct: Good pump-handle tail.

Incorrect; Too much curl.

GAIT AND MOVEMENT

Movement should be free, powerful and agile, with economy of effort. Legs should be moving parallel when viewed from front or rear, with discernible drive from the hindlegs. A dog's action is the way in which his limbs are employed to move him in his particular gait. The Stafford has his own style of movement, front legs moving neither wide nor narrow, and hindquarters moving parallel to them. There should be a rhythm and spring in the stride, and the animal has to be positive in his action and should not weave or high step. A Stafford with good shoulders and a well let down back-end is a joy to behold when he moves. Any Stafford who is loose at the shoulder, out at the elbow, upright in the shoulder or high in the hock cannot move in a typical manner. Always remember that without proper muscular training and ring training, you will not see the true action so typical of our breed.

MOVEMENT

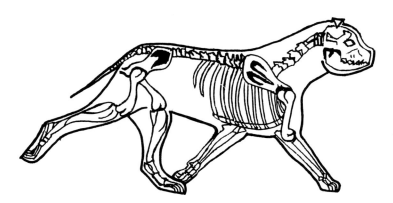

Skeletal illustration of correct movement. Good bone structure with correct layback of shoulder and deep chest. Free powerful stride coupled with economy of effort.

Correct movement in profile showing front extension and discernible drive from the hindlegs.

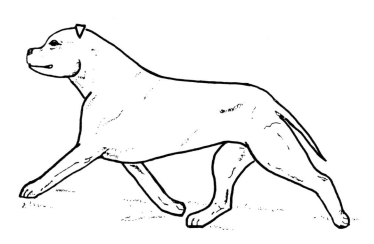

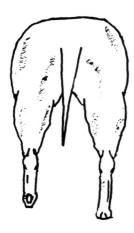

Correct movement viewed from the rear. The back legs are moving parallel to the front.

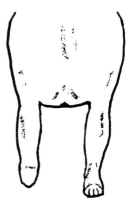

Correct movement viewed from the front. The forelegs are moving parallel with the hindlegs.

COAT

The Staffordshire Bull Terrier's coat should be smooth, short and close to the skin. Its texture is semi-harsh to the touch, and pleasant to handle. When the dog is angry, his muscles swell up and his coat covers him like a tight-fitting suit of armour. By doing this, he makes it harder for an adversary to get a hold of him. The dog's coat will tell you straight away if he is in good condition, as it should be smooth and have a glisten to it. There should be no coarse feeling or length to it, which often suggests that the dog has been kept in cold, draughty conditions. Staffords thrive in the home and this shows quite clearly in the showring, where you can always tell the difference between a dog who has been kennelled and one who lives in the house.

COLOUR

The colour of a Staffordshire Bull Terrier is a controversial subject. People argue about it continuously. The one colour that is much discussed is black-and-tan. Some people just cannot tell the difference between black-and-tan and tri-colour. If you stop and think about it, black-and-tan is two, and tri is three. It is as simple as that. The approved colours for Staffords are red, fawn, white, black or blue, and any of these colours with white, also any shade of brindle or any shade of brindle with white. Black-and-tan or liver are not to be encouraged. In fact, in the USA black-and-tan or liver dogs are disqualified from the show ring.

In the red colour we like to see a dark mask and black toenails. When judging, one should use one's discretion and not be too hard on an animal with lots going for it but whose colour is not a hundred per cent. Always remember that colour could not help the Stafford as a fighting dog.

I have heard some say that the blue colour came from the Blue Paul, but I fail to see on what basis they could claim this, except for the fact that the colour is the same. Just to put the record straight, there is no connection whatsoever between the colour blue in the Stafford and the Blue Paul. Genetically, blue, fawn, black and brindle are the same colour. You only have to look at some of the breeds where these colours predominate – Great Danes, Whippets, Greyhounds, Shar Peis, and so on. All carry the colour blue to the fore, and even the old Sourmug himself, the Bulldog, is capable of producing these colours. If there is a common ancestral dog for colour, then I am sure the Bulldog would be a more likely top candidate.

As far as the black-and-tan is concerned, the reason why this colour is so frowned on could be to

Liver-coloured puppies, like this Austrian-born pair with strong Rendorn and Linestaff breeding behind them, are produced from time to time. However, this colour is strongly faulted in the show ring.

do with the feet. On the black-and-tan Terrier (English Toy Terrier), the two middle toes on the front feet should be longer than the others, the back feet being cat-like. With such feet, there would be no grip on the surface to propel the dog across the pit. Because of this disadvantage, one can see why the old-timers did not want this colour in their breed. All the black-and-tans I have seen, no matter what their breeding, looked alike. It goes without saying that they are obviously very dominant for type, whether for colour or make and shape, and one of the most obvious faults was that the two outside toes on the front feet were shorter than the middle ones.

SIZE AND WEIGHT

The weight of dogs should be 28-38lbs, and bitches 24-34lbs. The desirable height at withers is 14-16 inches, these heights being related to the weights. In the early years there was a wide divergence of weights and sizes. Even in the 1930s, it was not unusual to see Staffords of 18lbs standing 16 inches high, and others of 19 inches tall weighing 50lbs. These days we have a more uniform size and weight. We are a bit more concessionary, allowing the most balanced dog to win, even if he is that little bit over the height or weight. The present desire among breeders seems to be to produce stocky, type-filled specimens. Hopefully we have seen the last of the small, low-legged, heavy-headed dogs that we saw in the late sixties and early seventies. The physical attributes with which our Staffords are endowed suit a dog of substance and size, capable of doing the job for which he was bred.

TERMINOLOGY USED WHEN DESCRIBING THE STAFFORD

ALMOND EYES: The eye set in surrounding tissue of almond shape.

APPLE HEAD: Very domed, rounded skull.

BAD MOUTH: Crooked or unaligned teeth with a bite over- or undershot in excess of standard specifications.

BALANCE: A consistent whole: symmetrical, typically proportioned as a whole or as regards its separate parts: balance of head, balance of body, or balance of head and body.

BITE: The relative position of the upper and lower teeth when the mouth is closed. (See Level bite, Scissor bite, Undershot and Overshot.)

BONE: The relative size (girth) of a dog's leg-bones. (See Substance.)

BRINDLE: A fine, even mixture of black hairs and a lighter colour, usually red, brown or grey, with the black hairs assembled in bands.

BRISKET: The forepart of the body below the chest, between the forelegs, closest to the ribs.

BULL NECK: A short, thick, heavy neck.

BURR: The inside of the ear: i.e. the irregular formation visible within the cup.

BUTTERFLY NOSE: A parti-coloured nose: e.g. dark spotted with flesh colour.

CANINES: The two upper and lower sharp-pointed teeth next to the incisors; fangs.

CHEEK: Fleshy part of the head below the eyes and above the mouth.

CHIPPENDALE FRONT: Forelegs out at elbows, pasterns close and feet out.

CHOPS: Jowls or pendulous flesh of the lips and jaw.

CLODDY: Low, thickset, comparatively heavy.

CLOSE-COUPLED: Short in coupling.

COARSE: Lacking in refinement.

COBBY: Short-bodied, compact.

CONDITION: Health as shown by the coat, state of flesh, general appearance and deportment.

CONFORMATION: The form and structure, make and shape; arrangement of the parts in conformity with Breed Standard demands.

COUPLING: That part of the body between the last ribs and the hip joints joined by the backbone.

COW-HOCKED: When the hocks turn inward towards each other.

CRABBING: Dog moves with his body at an angle to the line of travel.

CRYPTORCHID: The adult male whose testicles are abnormally retained in the abdominal cavity. Bilateral cryptorchidism involves both sides, that is, neither testicle has descended into the scrotum. Unilateral cryptorchidism involves one side only.

DENTITION: The number and arrangement of the teeth. Every dog should have a complete set of 42.

DISH FACED: When the nasal bone is so formed that the nose is higher at the tip than the stop.

DOMED: Evenly rounded in skull; convex instead of flat.

DOWN-FACED: The muzzle inclining downwards from the skull to the tip of the nose.

DOWN ON PASTERN: Weak or faulty pastern (metacarpus) set at a pronounced angle from the vertical.

DRIVE: A solid thrusting at the hindquarters, denoting sound locomotion.

DUDLEY NOSE: Flesh, brown or putty coloured nose.

ELBOWS (Out at the): Turning out or off from the body; not held close.

EXPRESSION: The general appearance of all features of the head as viewed from the front.

FLYING EARS: Any characteristic drop ears or semi-prick ears that stand or 'fly'.

FOREFACE: The front part of the head, before the eyes; muzzle.

FRONT: The forepart of the body as viewed head on, i.e. forelegs, chest, brisket and shoulder line.

GAY TAIL: The tail carried very high.

HEIGHT: Vertical measurement from the withers to the ground; referred to usually as shoulder height. (See Withers.)

HOCKS WELL LET DOWN: Hock joints close to the ground.

LEGGY: Too long in the leg for correct balance.

LEVEL BACK: The line of the back horizontal or parallel to the ground.

LEVEL BITE: When the front teeth (incisors) of the upper and lower jaws meet exactly edge to edge. Pincer bite (often referred to as a flush mouth).

LIPPY: Pendulous lip or lips that do not fit tightly.

LOADED SHOULDERS: When the shoulder blades are pushed out from the body by over-development of the muscles.

LONG COUPLED: Opposite to short coupled; having a long loin.

LOW SET: When tail is set on below level of topline, or when ears are set too low for correct placement for the breed.

MASK: Dark shading on the foreface.

MONORCHID: A dog with only one testicle.

MOVING CLOSE: When the hind limbs move close to each other, through complete length of limb remaining straight.

MUZZLE: The head in front of the eyes.

OCCIPUT: Upper, back point of skull.

OUT AT SHOULDER: With shoulder blades loosely attached to the body, leaving the shoulders jutting out in relief and increasing the breadth of the front.

OVERSHOT: The front teeth (incisors) of the upper jaw overlap and do not touch the front teeth of the lower jaw when the mouth is closed.

PADDLING: The front feet thrown out sideways in a loose, uncontrolled manner.

PIED: A term used for a dog having two colours in unusual proportions; mainly white with large patches of black or brindle colouring placed irregularly over the body. (White and red is known as skewbald.)

PLAITING: Manner of walking or trotting in which the legs cross.

PRICK EARS: Carried erect and pointed at the tip.

RACY: Tall, long-bodied dog of comparatively slight build.

RED: Strictly speaking, this is a general term for several colours, ranging from fawn to copper-red.

ROLLING GAIT: Swaying, ambling action when moving.

ROSE EAR: A small drop ear which folds over and back, so as to reveal the burr.

SCISSOR BITE: Jaws strong, with a perfect, regular and complete scissor bite, i.e. the upper teeth closely overlapping the lower teeth and set square to the jaws. (Often referred to as a level mouth.)

SCREW TAIL: A naturally short tail twisted in a more or less spiral formation.

SET ON: Placement of tail on body; also position of ears on skull.

SHORT COUPLED: With very short coupling.

SNIPY: A pointed, weak muzzle.

SOUNDNESS: The state of mental and physical health when all organs and faculties are complete and functioning normally, each in its rightful relation to the others.

SPLAYFOOT: A flat foot with toes spreading, open foot, open toed.

STIFLE: The joint of the hind leg between the thigh and the second thigh, the dog's knee.

STILTED: Stiff, jerking gait.

STOP: The step-up from muzzle to skull.

STRAIGHT STIFLES: Stifle joint in which femur and tibia meet at an angle of approximately 180 degrees.

SUBSTANCE: Heaviness of bone and general volume of body.

TEMPERAMENT: Mixture of natural qualities and traits which produce character.

TUCK-UP: Concave underloin of body curving upward from depth of rib to narrow waist.

UNDERSHOT: The front teeth (incisors) of the lower jaw overlapping or projecting beyond the front teeth of the upper jaw when the mouth is closed.

WELL SPRUNG RIBS: Ribs springing out from spinal column giving good round shape.

WITHERS: The highest point of the body immediately behind the neck.

WRINKLE: Loose, folding skin on the forehead and face.

WRY MOUTH: Lower jaw does not line up with upper jaw (teeth on one side of mouth undershot).

Chapter Nine

IN THE SHOW RING

EARLY DAYS

Pride in possessing something better than your neighbour has always been a failing of human nature, and in no way has our ego been more evident than in showing dogs. Clean, healthy competition is harmless, and in the old days the relative merits of dogs were decided in a practical way: rat killing competitions, badger baiting, bull baiting, and dog fighting. By the early years of the nineteenth century it was realised that selective breeding was necessary to evolve the perfect dog for each canine sport, and at about the same period the scientific breeding of agricultural livestock was first developed. Along with this came the industrial revolution, shifting many people from country life to the busy life of the towns, and leaving them with little time for their old pursuits involving animals. At the same time, in 1835, the prohibition of cruel sports left the Bulldog and the Bull Terrier without a role in life.

In order to achieve success in the show ring, you must not only possess a top-class animal, you must also learn how to show the dog to advantage. I am pictured with Ashstock Scarlet Buttons, Best in Show winner at the 1991 Southern Counties Staffordshire Bull Terrier Club Championship show, with judges Tom Horner, Mick Clarke and Bruce Nicholls.

These various factors turned the thoughts of dog fanciers to competitions which would decide the relative merits of their dogs by judging them on their appearance, and by 1861 dog shows were firmly established in this country. At first, the dogs were judged by practical men who knew the working qualities and the conformation necessary to enable a dog to carry out its task in the field, pit or arena, and the dogs were assessed on these points. Then came breed specialist societies, who standardised the points and protected the various established breeds from further adulteration. Breed Standards were drawn up strictly on working qualities, and dog shows have certainly made the general public dog-conscious, and have increased the number of well-kept, well-bred dogs.

CHAMPIONSHIP SHOWS

In Britain all Championship shows are benched, which means that each breed has its own section of benching, usually clearly labelled, but stewards will assist exhibitors in finding their benching. Exhibitors must secure their dog with a chain on the correct bench. In the USA and many oher countries, benching is not used, and exhibitors present themselves at the appropriate breed ring at the correct time. Hard-working ring stewards endeavour to get all competitors in the ring at the correct time for their respective classes, but the exhibitor has only himself to blame if he misses his classes. Keep checking with your ring steward to make sure the time of judging has not been changed.

JUDGES

When in the ring the handler should pay attention to nothing but his own dog and take pains to keep his exhibit standing correctly and showing himself off to perfection. A wee bit of relaxation may be permitted if the handler is quite certain the judge is looking the other way, but he should keep watching out of the corner of his eye to make sure the judge does not make a sudden turn to have another look at the dog, perhaps to compare him with one on the opposite side of the ring.

THE JUDGING PROCEDURE

The judge approaches each dog individually for a detailed examination.

Nash.

The mouth is checked to see if the dog has full dentition and the correct scissor bite required for the breed.

Nash.

The judge then moves down the dog looking at the head, the forequarters, the body and the hindquarters.

Nash.

The judge's instructions regarding moving the dog in a certain direction and standing in a certain place must be strictly obeyed, and the dog must be instantly removed from the ring if so ordered. Most judges are exceedingly sympathetic towards novices, and a quiet word at the bar, or other convenient meeting place, after all the judging has finished, will bring forth a considered explanation of where your exhibit, or your showmanship, was weak.

Exhibits are not permitted to leave the venue before a certain time, and if they do, it must be with the written permission of the Show secretary. This permission should only be requested in cases of extreme necessity, as absences are not fair on the public, who have paid for admittance to the show in order to look round the exhibits, and who do not appreciate finding the benches half empty.

The judge will then ask the handler to move the dog to assess movement, firstly from the rear.   *Nash.*

Movement from the front is assessed as the handler moves back towards the judge. In the UK the triangular pattern of movement is favoured which allows the judge to see the dog from the rear, in profile, and from the front.   *Nash.*

HANDLING

We are lucky that our breed is in the hands of enthusiastic talented amateurs. With no 'professional handlers' as such, showing and breeding provides an interesting hobby, with reasonable chances for anyone with the necessary ability and time. When your young charge goes to his first show he will be required to move in straight line across the ring to and from the judge so that his action may be assessed. All the work that you have put in with that little bit of extra training should pay dividends for you — training whereby he has progressed to the point where he will stand at command and is going well on the lead. All his practice in walking at a steady pace from one point to another in a direct line, turning and returning in the same way, will now seem worthwhile. This may seem a very simple performance, but anyone who has judged will know how many exhibits spoil their chances of being included among the winners by pulling hard on the lead, wavering from side to side, or slinking along the ground with the tail down when called on to move across the ring. A dog that goes boldly and under good control on a lead during a walk in the open may disgrace himself and his owner in the show ring, unless trained to move in the manner suggested in a confined space.

It is a common mistake to confine show training to the vicinity of the kennel or garden. The aim is to teach the dog aspiring to show honours to display and move to the best advantage, in what will be, for the Stafford, unfamiliar and perhaps rather nerve-testing surroundings. He will be

A study in concentration: Ch. Boldmore Black Sabbath with owner Mick Clarke. All dogs must learn to stand correctly in the show ring. Stacking is customary in the breed; the Stafford is placed in the correct position by the handler and posed for the judge.

Expert handling: Sharon Fletcher with Dumbriton Special Brew at Berlscarg, judged by international Stafford expert, Terry Giles.

excited or worried by unaccustomed noises, sights and scents, and bustled about among strange dogs and people. Home training should, therefore, be supplemented by lessons in a park, square, or street, so that the dog may learn to perform in the face of all kinds of distractions. If a puppy is kept away from crowds, traffic noises and novel experiences, it cannot be expected to be bold and full of itself when taken into a show ring and handled by strangers. If your home is in a quiet, secluded district, the youngster should be allowed to accompany you on shopping expeditions to the nearest town, or be taken on a journey by car, bus or train, and generally brought into contact with crowds, strange dogs, sudden noises and other disturbing factors.

Berlscarg Black Crystal: Winner of Best Puppy Bitch at her first Championship Show – a classic example of doing your homework with your puppy before taking it to a show.

A natural showman: Ch. Pitmax Pasidion of Dumbriton, aged ten months, posing without assistance from the handler. This Stafford made breed history when he won his title in a record ten days. He went on to win a total of ten CCs and seven Reserve CCs.

STACKING

In the ring, how does the judge want the dog to stand to his best advantage? Some owners may well ask themselves that question, judging from some of the positions we see dogs placed in from time to time. To stand a dog up, or as some say to stack him, there are certain fundamental points to observe. Get these correct and the rest will all fall into line. Firstly, the hocks, i.e. the hind legs. These are, as it were, the anchors, and must at all times be absolutely perpendicular to the ground, forming a right angle, leaning neither forward nor backward. Get the hocks into position first, then place your dog's front legs so they are directly underneath him, with elbows close to the brisket. When you have got your Stafford into this position, you can put your finger under the dog's chin. This maintains contact, and at the same time you can pull slightly up on his lead to lift the head, gently pulling down on the loose skin under the chin. All these movements should be made while talking to your dog, and reassuring him that he is doing well. By talking, I do not mean just verbally: I talk to my dogs with my hands. I will not go into great detail, but I am convinced, through many years of experience, that it is quite possible, and indeed desirable, to communicate your thoughts to a dog through touch. Actually, although they may not realise this, nearly everyone 'knows' it even if they have never seriously thought about it.

HANDLING FAULTS

Some handlers in the breed are excellent, while others are very poor, and the following "don'ts" may be helpful. It does not matter whether you prefer to show your dog by standing in front of him, or at the back (the old-fashioned way, as I call it), or whether you prefer to kneel at his side. I prefer to show most dogs from the front. By doing so, I always feel I have more control over the exhibit and am able to see the whole of the dog with very little effort. What is more, I can get a good view from above and in addition, the dog can see me: he knows me in this position and can thus have confidence and relax – and here we have the whole secret.

One of the things very much commented on in the breed these days is movement. When getting your puppy to go on the lead, you will obviously have taken every opportunity to watch his movement, both fore and aft. You will no doubt have had him 'walked up' for you by someone else, while you watched from behind, in front and from the side. There is nothing you can do about improving movement – it is either there or it is not – but when you are moving your dog in the ring, never position yourself between your dog and the judge. Few things are more annoying to a judge, who is trying to see the best in your dog, than for you to keep getting between him (or her) and your exhibit, thus hindering a correct decision.

There is no real problem in handling if, as I say, common sense is used. Just observe the few hints I have given you, and I am sure you will find that all goes well. Don't get flustered, and remember that any judge likes a calm exhibitor who quietly and quickly carries out what is required. Also bear in mind that any judge worthy of the name will always allow an obvious novice all the time in the world to get settled and relaxed in the ring.

SELECTING A SHOW PUPPY

If I were asked what particular phase of my 'doggy' activities gives me the greatest thrill, I think I should say choosing the pick of the litter. As far as I am concerned, there is nothing quite so interesting as to take a litter and quietly examine each puppy, thinking ahead all the time about what it is likely to achieve when it is fully mature. Will it bring you yet another Champion to your kennel? Will it breed you one if you are thinking in terms of building up a strong kennel? Or will it be one to have a bit of fun with around the local Open shows? And so on.

Competition in Staffordshire Bull Terriers today is so keen that most topline decisions by first-

It takes a skilled and experienced eye to pick out a potential show winner from a litter of young puppies. This eight-week-old red puppy shows plenty of bone and substance, strong hindquarters, well-bent stifle and well let down hocks.

Viewed from the front, the same puppy shows a strong head, well-placed eyes, good bone and a correct front.

Jodel's Great Expectations and Jodel's Red Delight: Two beautifully bred puppies who went on to make their mark in South Africa

rate judges of the breed are of a knife-edge variety, so we must approach our task of selection very carefully. First of all, make up your mind what you want and stick to it – do not be talked out of your original intentions. It is beneficial if you have knowledge of the sire or dam, and maybe even a fleeting knowledge of those further back in the pedigree. Study the puppies' pedigree carefully before you even have a look at the dogs themselves. For the purpose of these few hints, let us assume that would-be buyers of a puppy know little or nothing about the breed, but that they have assured themselves that the youngsters are correctly bred.

It is quite right to say that Staffordshire Bull Terriers breed true to type nowadays, and this is where some knowledge of their pedigree will be of the greatest importance. However, although the majority who have a passing knowledge of the breed invariably claim that they are an easy breed and the selection of a puppy is a simple matter, nothing can be further from the truth. When you visit the litter, first of all, and this is important, have a good look at the place where the puppies are housed. Size up the breeder and try to form some idea about his feeding methods and so on. Having satisfied yourself that the puppies have been sensibly and comfortably reared to date, turn your attention to the puppies themselves. Not forgetting that the pedigree must play a big part in their ultimate development, go into detail regarding how they are bred. I am no believer in the 'chance puppy', but contend that like comes from like nine times out of ten.

Make no mistake – the breed today is definitely not slipping. Staffords are undoubtedly far better

Judges base their results on their own personal interpretation of the Breed Standard, and so many years of experience is needed before you take on this role. I am pictured judging a Championship show in South Africa in 1992.

than they have ever been as a show proposition, and the breed has a much wider appeal than it has hitherto enjoyed. Anyone who claims the opposite simply labels himself as either prejudiced or very ignorant of the modern-day Stafford. If the breed has a main fault nowadays, I would say it is in movement. Therefore, when bearing the sire and dam in mind, think also about how they moved in the ring, for action is terribly hereditary. How do you estimate movement when it is obvious that a young puppy cannot be taken on a lead and seen to advantage? This is where knowledge of the sire and dam comes in, for one thing. Another good plan is to let your selected puppy run free and to watch him at play. Faulty movement will soon be detected, and, likewise, sound movement plainly seen. I will only reiterate that Staffordshire Bull Terriers usually breed true to type. Keep that in mind and remember what I have tried to outline and you will not go far wrong – in fact you won't go wrong at all, and you may pick yourself a future Champion.

Chapter Ten

THE THEORY OF DOG BREEDING

Dog breeding is a combination of art and science, with the added ingredients of the breeder's skill, expertise and boundless optimism – plus a good share of luck. In many cases, breeding programmes have been started almost by accident. A dog is bought for a pet, and, by sheer luck, someone in the breed spots the Stafford and encourages the owner to start showing. A few successes in the show ring follow, and if the Stafford is a bitch, the next step is to mate her and to try rearing a litter. If the Stafford is a male, it is not long before the novice show-goer is planning to buy a bitch. So, more often than not, it is a much-loved bitch, originally bought as a pet, that is the foundation of a breeding programme. How long an individual remains involved in the dog world depends on personal preference and the success of the kennel. However, although many have found that it is very difficult to start a programme of breeding good dogs, it is almost impossible to stop once you have started!

GETTING STARTED

It can be seen, then, that the majority of breeders do not start their kennels with an outstanding animal, unless they are particularly lucky. If a breeder decides to switch from one breed to another, or to add another to their kennel, they are generally more successful as they set about acquiring their foundation stock with a degree of knowledge and skill.

Do not get involved with dog breeding if you have plans to make a lucrative business from it. By the time you have paid a stud fee, veterinary fees, the feeding costs of the bitch and the puppies, and possibly advertising to sell the puppies, you will probably have used up all your profit margin. The reward of breeding dogs is to produce sound, healthy specimens of the breed, and to place them in good, caring homes. If dogs carrying your kennel name go on to win in the show ring, that should be regarded as a bonus. A breeder should never take their wins or their disappointments too seriously.

The science of inheritance is extremely complicated; there are exceptions to all rules, and there are many unknown quantities. The average dog breeder has neither the time nor the inclination to undertake an in-depth study of genetics. However, there are a number of excellent books that have been written on the subject, which could be studied to advantage. Even if the breeder does not want to get involved with learning all the complicated terms involved in genetics, it is important to acquire a basic understanding of the theory of inheritance.

There are breeders who produce good dogs purely by planning a programme based on commonsense, personal observations and years of experience. However, this experience will be gained far more slowly than if it was based on an understanding of why particular faults and virtues have been perpetuated. There are faults in every breeding line, but with careful, selective

Irish Ch. Lasanta Dark Divinity (right) and Irish Ch. Ebony Jen: It is important to understand the laws of genetics in order to be a successful breeder of dogs.

breeding they can be minimised or even eliminated – and this is for the good of the breed as a whole.

UNDERSTANDING GENETICS

The name genetics comes from the Greek word 'genos', meaning a race. This rapidly growing branch of biological science is possibly *the* most important, as it deals with life itself.

Genes are the hereditary factors that are passed from the parent to the offspring; they are the physical 'links' that are passed from one generation to the next. Each individual has thousands of genes, and they are transmitted as the entire inheritance. A string of beads is often used as the most simple way of explaining the bodies of chromosomes that carry the genes.

Both the male and the female carry the same number of chromosomes, which occur in pairs. The offspring inherits the chromosomes, the pairs being made up with one part from the male and one part from the female. Thus inheritance comes equally from both parents. However, this may not be represented in the physical appearance or character of the individual offspring, because it depends which of the inherited factors dominate. That is why individual members of the same litter may look very different from each other even though their parentage is the same. In essence, the science of genetics is understanding why certain factors are inherited in certain ways.

The vast majority of living organisms owe their existence to the union of two individuals of different sexes. It is the meeting of the minute sperm of the male with the egg of the female at fertilisation which produces each new individual. Theoretically, the union of two cells should give a double cell, twice the size of the two cells which formed it, with double the contents, i.e. a full set of genes and chromosomes from each parent. However the sperm and the egg are, in effect, half-cells, and the full quota of the offspring's genes are chromosomes made up as a result of cell division.

Before fertilisation takes place, the chromosome and genes divide, with one member from each pair going to form the individual offspring, and a corresponding half coming from the other parent. The contribution from each parent is a sample half of their own inheritance.

MENDELIAN GENETICS

Genes combine in many ways, and in some gene pairs, one member is able to suppress the effect of its partner. This was the first genetic discovery made by the great Gregor Johann Mendel (1822-1884), who is known as the Father of Genetics.

Ch. Bekanbar Barolo: External factors such as rearing also play a part in the development of offspring.

Raymond.

When Mendel was twenty-one he became a novice in an Augustinian monastery and was ordained in 1847. For some years he attended the university of Vienna, and then returned to his monastery. Between 1857 and 1868, when he became Abbot, Mendel worked on a series of experiments using peas, grown in the monastery garden. From his experiments he discovered the laws of heredity, finding out how characteristics are transmitted. His findings were published in a paper issued by the Natural History Society in 1865. Unfortunately, the importance of Mendel's discovery was not recognised until 1902 – eighteen years after his death.

In a simplified form, Mendel discovered that when two individuals with contrasting traits are united/mated, one trait will appear in the offspring, and the other will not. He called the trait which shows, 'dominant, and the trait which does not appear, 'recessive'. Using his experiments with peas, Mendel was able to predict the appearance of resulting plants on the basis of which traits would be inherited. For example, he could accurately forecast which would be tall plants, which would be short plants, or which would have wrinkled peas or smooth peas, and what colour they would be. It is the application of this theory which is of importance to all breeders of livestock.

The dominant-recessive relationship is the cause of many hereditary characteristics, and this is the reason why particular faults and virtues are inherited. However, genes can work in many different and more complicated ways. Some can suppress the action of genes with which they are not paired, others can be suppressed. If they are suppressers they are termed 'distatic', if they are suppressed they are 'hypostatic'. Some genes can modify the effect of other genes. Single pairs of genes can produce their own effect, while in other cases, groups of genes may be needed to produce effects.

EXTERNAL INFLUENCES
The inheritance of characteristics cannot be separated from external influences. This starts from the pre-natal period, right through to the time the individual reaches full mental and physical maturity. Growth is a prime example of the action of the environment on heredity. The hereditary pattern for growth may be entirely favourable, but if the dog is starved of food, or not given food of sufficient quality or amount for its needs, the hereditary pattern will be hampered, and proper growth and development will not take place. On the other hand, the best rearing environment will not correct a poor hereditary pattern of growth.

BLOODLINES
The term 'bloodlines' has no exact meaning. It does not mean that inheritance, even of the closest relatives, need be entirely similar – except in the case of identical twins, which are the product of a single fertilised egg. Genes, as we have seen, are distributed among the offspring at random, and so it is possible for two littermates to vary considerably in their inheritance. However, related dogs are more likely to be alike, in spite of the random distribution of genes among progeny. They are more likely to possess genes in common, because of the close relationship. On the other hand, littermates may show differing characteristics because the sample each received from each parent may be quite different, on account of the separation of gene pairs at the time of mating and their re-combination in the next generation.

Genes do not blend in the process of reproduction: each maintains its own identity and is passed on, unchanged, with every generation. The sole exception is when a mutation occurs. This is a sudden, usually permanent, change in a gene, which alters its effect so that the organism is different from the normal. Mutations are rare, and can be the result of external factors such as the effect of radiation. The long-term effect of this type of gene depends on how it is paired in future unions.

TEMPERAMENT

This is an inherited characteristic, and is, perhaps, *the* most important one when it comes to breeding dogs. A fundamentally nervous temperament must be regarded as hereditary. It is true that nervousness in Staffordshire Bull terriers, as in other breeds, may be brought about by bad management and rough handling, but the Stafford who has inherited an unsound temperament is nervous from the very beginning, and remains so, however well the dog may be treated.

Fortunately, this type of dog is rare in the breed, but they are a pitiful sight. Small puppies will display fear for no reason, and will fail to respond to friendly advances. In later life, such a dog will be terrified of everyday experiences and encounters, which the normal Staffordshire Bull Terrier with a typical, happy disposition would take in its stride. This type of temperament is a major handicap to a pet dog, as it is to a show dog. Every effort should be made to eliminate unsound stock from a breeding programme. This is true of all animals which carry faults, but there is no doubt that a bad temperament is the worst fault of all.

Chapter Eleven

BREEDING STAFFORDS

The reasons that prompt people to embark on the fascinating adventure of breeding dogs are many and varied. It may be that a bitch puppy, originally acquired purely as a pet, becomes so handsome and dearly loved as she matures that the desire to produce others like her becomes irresistible. Or the spectacle of a number of beautifully presented Staffordshire Bull Terriers parading at a dog show may fire the spectator with a desire to breed similar specimens good enough to win top awards in the show ring.

BREEDING TO AN IDEAL
The breeder who seeks to win at shows, or who hopes to establish a successful train of potential winners, must always keep in the mind's eye the ideal Staffordshire Bull Terrier, as depicted by the official breed standard. They must strive patiently to produce stock which approaches this ideal more closely in each succeeding generation. The desire to breed strong, healthy, intelligent puppies free from hereditary weakness, either physical or temperamental, will be equally strong. In this sense too, they must breed to an ideal and will succeed or fail in their aims according to whether they take the trouble to understand and apply the basic laws which govern Staffordshire Bull Terrier reproduction in all its phases. Unfortunately, a novice breeder who sets out with high hopes and enthusiasm is sometimes sadly disappointed when the litter arrives. Such a situation is almost inevitable if the method adopted is to acquire a bitch at random and to mate her to the first good-looking dog that they set their eyes on. The breeding of pedigree stock can never be raised to an exact science, but a clever breeder should be able to forecast with reasonable confidence what to expect from any carefully planned mating. Until comparatively recently, dog breeders had to rely on rule-of-thumb methods, plus whatever could be gained from observation, experience, and commonsense. Today things are different. The laws which govern heredity are pretty well understood, and there is no longer any reason why the production of sound, typical, high-quality Staffordshire Bull Terriers should have to depend on the luck of the draw.

When we mate two animals we do so in the hope that certain desired qualities or characteristics will be transmitted by one or both of them to their offspring. In all serious breeding operations we set out to control the hereditary make-up of the puppies in the litters produced. If the bitch is weak in some point, the obvious course is to try to offset that failing by putting her to a dog especially good in that respect, in the hope that the sire's influence will correct the maternal fault in the puppies. It must be said, however, that this system does not always work out as expected.

IN-BREEDING
There are few subjects which breeders discuss more often or with greater fervour than the part

breeding can play in the improvement of type in pedigree dogs. The opinions expressed as regards the value or danger of in-breeding as compared with line-breeding, outcrossing and so on, show the widest divergences. Some breeders look upon the system as representing an evil to be avoided at all costs, contending that it must bring disaster and ruin in its wake. Others claim it is the only sure road to success for those whose aim is to build up a strain which can be relied on to breed true for the breed points required.

It is, however, as illogical to contend that in itself in-breeding is a malignant force as it is to claim it as a sovereign remedy for all the difficulties which lie in the breeder's path. In-breeding is simply a means of sorting out the virtues and faults inherent in a strain or family. Whether its results are good or bad depends entirely on the type of stock subjected to its influence, and the care with which it is applied.

Although such words as in-breeding, line-breeding and outcrossing are in constant use in discussions on 'doggy' matters, the terms are often used very loosely and are frequently misunderstood. In the widest sense, in-breeding consists of the inter-mating of relatives, and it is virtually impossible to breed pedigree stock of any kind without having recourse to it. As a rule, however, the term is used in a more restricted sense, to indicate the mating of such close relatives as mother and son, sire and daughter, or brother and sister. The breeding together of more distantly related individuals such as cousins, uncle and niece, half-brother and half-sister and so on, is referred to as line-breeding. Many people who are strongly opposed to in-breeding are great advocates of line-breeding, yet there is no essential difference between the two. Line-breeding is merely a milder, or less intense, form of in-breeding.

Genetically most of the points we seek to obtain in show stock are represented by dominant genes, while the unwanted characteristics, which we call faults, are produced by recessive genes. In any breed of dogs, two near relatives are likely to have more genes in common than two unrelated individuals, and the closer their relationship, the more alike genetically they are likely to be. The most direct method of producing genetic purity in a strain is, therefore, by in-breeding. But it must be remembered that genetic purity applies to faults as well as to virtues. In-breeding will fix both good and bad points, and will bring to light any weakness or defect which may be dormant in the parents. The first visual results of in-breeding may, therefore, be disappointing.

Litters born to an in-bred mating may show some, possibly many, faults which were not apparent in either of the parents, but the genes for the development of those defects must have been carried by both sire and dam. In-breeding cannot create either good or bad points, it can only make visible what is already present, albeit hidden, in the animals that are mated. It is a common fallacy to suppose that such failings as loss of vigour, weak pigmentation, impotence, sterility, susceptibility to infection, mental degeneration, loss of size, or bad temperament can originate through in-breeding. If these or any other defects appear in in-bred stock, it is because the parents carry the hereditary factors responsible for these conditions. The emergence of faults through the coming together of recessive genes can, of course, also occur in litters bred from unrelated parents, but in-breeding certainly increases the risk.

Any characteristics, whether physical or mental, can be fixed in, or eliminated from, a strain by in-breeding. Physical or constitutional strength, fertility, fearlessness, size or high intelligence and trainability may be in-bred into a strain, as surely as such points as length of head, ear shape, eye colour or coat texture. This fact is very apt to be ignored by those who regard in-breeding as being inevitably associated with degeneration. If the early results of in-breeding are disappointing, the remedy is not to go over to outcrossing, but to continue to inbreed, with drastic weeding out of all faulty progeny as it appears. The main reason breeders with only slight experience of in-breeding often decry it, is that they have failed to persevere long enough for the benefits which might have been derived to become apparent. It is also a common mistake to lack ruthlessness in discarding all faulty or weak puppies in the litter bred. If vigorous culling is practised in the early stages, in-bred stock will become increasingly more uniform both genetically and in appearance in later generations, so that a true breeding line of high-quality, typical animals may be established.

It is useless to embark on a programme of in-breeding with chance-bred or mediocre stock. At every mating, the animals chosen must be of high quality and free from any serious hereditary defects. Unless material of this calibre is available, efforts should be concentrated on building up a stock of sound, typical, individuals by outcrossing, line-breeding and selection. The object of in-breeding is to produce a strain of animals all conforming closely to a desired pattern. The longer in-breeding is continued, the more alike its products will become. In time, it will be effective in fixing all the qualities inherent in a strain, both good and bad. If selection is applied with care and within wide enough limits in each generation, only the good points will be stabilised, but if faults are overlooked or ignored in the animals bred from, they too will be fixed in the strain and further in-breeding will cause deterioration.

Much has been written on the subject of in-breeding, most of it going right over the head of the novice. It is the old story: theory does not always work out in practice. It never ceases to amaze me how 'near' we can go without in any way impairing the breed. For instance, father to daughter more often than not gives good results, whereas son to mother matings are invariably poor. Brother and sister matings are dangerous and not to be recommended, while grandfather to grand-daughter is one that a lot of breeders swear by. As breeders, we have always stuck by half-brother to half-sister as our most successful mating. I know that some enthusiasts will argue that this is more like line-breeding, and I would agree with them, if it had only happened once! But we would do it for two or three generations, and I think it goes without saying that our Dumbriton type is very distinct, and can be easily picked out in the show ring.

LINE-BREEDING

In line-breeding, the mated animals are not so closely related, which means that the resemblance of offspring to parents will probably be less strongly marked than in closely in-bred stock. Genetic purity and physical uniformity will also take longer to achieve, but though line-breeding is slower in fixing desirable qualities than in-breeding, it is also less likely to expose faults. For that reason, where immediate results are of more importance than the ultimate establishment of a genuine true-breeding strain, it may be considered preferable and safer than in-breeding. It should, however, be understood that anything which may be gained through line-breeding may be obtained more quickly and more directly by in-breeding. The point to bear in mind is that the higher the general quality of a strain, the closer it may be in-bred without ill effects, always providing that precautions are taken to weed out every puppy which fails to come up to a required standard. To attempt to initiate a programme of in-breeding with inferior stock or to continue with it when a fault shows signs of becoming fixed in the strain is to court certain disaster.

OUTCROSSING

An outcross, in other words the breeding together of two unrelated animals, should only be made for a special purpose. The belief that a change of blood must in all cases be salutary after in-breeding has been practised for a few generations is mistaken. If, through lack of care in selection, or from other causes, a recessive fault becomes widespread in a strain, it may be necessary to resort to an outcross in order to bring in the dominant gene to correct it. The snag is that, however carefully the animal to be used as an outcross is chosen, he is almost certain to bring in not only the genes desired, but other factors that are not wanted. He will probably be genetically impure for

Ch. Rapparee Rothersykes Vow: This top-winning male went on to become a highly influential stud dog and is strongly behind the well-known Wyrefare and Spadille kennels.

several of the qualities for which a high degree of genetic purity has been established in the line into which he is to be crossed, so that certain recessive genes will be passed on to any progeny sired by him. An outcross should be regarded as an experiment, and in a well-established strain should not be made without good reason.

There are times when outcrossing may be imperative, as when a fault or weakness occurs repeatedly in members of a certain family or strain, but every effort should be made to see that the animal used brings in as few alien traits, or genetic impurities, as possible. The best way to ensure this is to try to find an individual which, though not closely related, carries some of the same foundation bloodlines as the strain with which it is to be crossed. In a small or numerically weak breed, that may not be feasible, but in the more popular varieties like Staffordshire Bull Terriers a breeder resorting to indirect line-breeding, as opposed to in-breeding in the restricted sense, may be able to obtain the desired results with less risk than by a more dramatic outcross. Having made an outcross, the next step is to breed back strongly to the original line. Except in very exceptional circumstances, this is the only safe course to follow, once the purpose of outcrossing has been achieved. Only in this way can the genetic purity previously established in a valuable strain be maintained.

LINE AND FAMILY BREEDING
This is one of the best methods of breeding that you can use, because it brings into play the

Germ. Ch. High Jaker vom Brindle King: A prolific winner in the show ring who has been largely responsible for establishing the breed in Germany.

Family breeding: Ch. Juna vom Brindle King with Tochter Ninja vom Brindle King.

strength you must place in your bitch line. You can use the best stud dog in the country to a third-rate bitch and possibly get a winner from this mating, but — and it is a big but — it will not breed on. In the last few years, we have had in the breed a top winning dog who has been used extensively at stud, and to date has only produced two or three good animals from about 100 matings. I personally felt, at the time the dog became a Champion, that he would never make a good stud dog, for the simple reason that he was, in my opinion, a nonentity. In other words, he had no great virtues and no great faults, and was out of a second-rate bitch. He is a perfect example of what can happen if specimens are not strongly line-bred, since without strong virtues they cannot be expected to make good sires. Bear in mind the old saying 'You can't make a silk purse out of a sow's ear.' Always remember that the bitch is the all-important anchor in your breeding programme, because without a first-rate, linebred bitch you are wasting your time, as you can freely have the pick of the best stud dogs in the country.

The line and family system, as I have said, is considered a certain way to produce good stock, and the method of using particular lines is ilustrated in the pedigree of Ch. Skerry Dhu of Dumbriton. Mr H.M. Beilby, in 1935, was a great advocate of this system. He set up the method of 'Families and Lines' in Staffords. This was quite easy to do in those days, as the breed was in its infancy as far as pedigrees and registrations were concerned. Beilby was able to work out six different lines and the importance of these lines was identified by the dogs who were their founders, i.e. the main dog of each line in question.

			Ch Nethertonion Storm Trooper
		Spadille Sammy Spade	
			Black Magic Of Spadille
	Spadille Netherdale Pride Of Barons		
			Ch Skean Dhu
		Spadille Sunday Best	
			Black Magic Of Spadille
Dumbriton Jack To A King			
			Vencristo Domino
		Donellas Rockafella	
			Dennybeck Double Time
	Magliam Brazen Bess Of Dumbriton		
			Ch Swinfen Sky Scraper
		Pitmax Brazen Lady	
			Lady Red Samba
CH SKERRY DHU OF DUMBRITON			
			Ch Nethertonion Storm Trooper
		Spadille Sammy Spade	
			Black Magic Of Spadille
	Spadille Netherdale Pride Of Barons		
			Ch Skean Dhu
		Spadille Sunday Best	
			Black Magic Of Spadille
Lady Emma Of Balstruan			
			Berts Pal Of Rothersyke
		Spadille Seannachie	
			Spartan Spadille
	Marojo Sundae Girl		
			Bionic Boy
		Dalmejo Dazzler	
			Blinkbonny Of Dalmejo

Ch. Skerry Dhu Of Dumbriton: This illustrates family or line breeding.

THE BROOD BITCH

Whether you have bought your bitch puppy as a pet or for showing, in time she will have a season. This normally occurs when she is about six months old, and her second season will normally come six months after the first. In a breed like Staffordshire Bull Terriers, bitches are usually mated at their second season when they are fully mature, both physically and mentally.

The best thing to do if you want to have a litter of puppies is to take the young bitch to her breeder, who will advise you if she is good enough to mate. The one thing breeders do not want is for a bitch of their breeding to be mated if she does not reach the required high standard they breed for. She does not have to be a top-class bitch, in other words a Champion or a CC winner, but she must have the most important thing in any breed – and that is breed type. She must be a typial specimen of the breed with no outstanding faults; she must be sound in temperament and she must have a clean bill of health.

THE STUD DOG

It is not always necessary to run a stud dog when starting to found a kennel – in fact it is far better to leave well alone at the outset. The careful selection of the stud dog must, however, be high on your priority as step number two. Having bought your brood bitch you now have something to go at, as it were. You know her breeding and you should by now have some idea of the various dogs that are standing at stud, and what they have produced when mated to bitches carrying the same bloodlines as your own bitch. We have a well-known saying in Staffords that you should never use a 'bitchy' stud dog — always use a dog that 'has plenty of give'. It does not make any difference even if he is a Champion, as that fact does not guarantee his success at stud.

When you acquire your brood bitch do not, with your limited knowledge, immediately start to think of using an outcross. I have seen so many examples of good bitches from well-established kennels being taken to an outcross stud by a novice owner, and the resulting litter being very poor quality. Look at outcrossing in the way a chef would look at producing the perfect soup. He will spend hours and hours adding a little of this and a little of that, simmering and tasting and so on, until he decides that it has got his trademark for quality. It may then be served at the table to a man who, before he has even tasted it, stretches out his hand for the strongest sauce he can find and dollops in a great spoonful, thus ruining all the care and thought the chef has put into the making of the soup. This is just what the experimenter in outcrossing does when he decides to found a 'new bloodline'.

So think what you are doing when looking for the sire of your first litter. I would strongly advise that when you buy your brood bitch you obtain all the details of her breeding, and ask the vendor who he would recommend as a suitable mate in her next season. Nine times out of ten he will give you some excellent advice, and if he suggests one of his own stud dogs, do not immediately jump to wrong conclusions. The seller is probably giving you the very best advice and, possibly, had you not bought her, he would have carried out that same mating with excellent results. Gain all the knowledge you can, but before you make your final decision, have a good look around and see what you can discover from show catalogues and so on. Investigate the results of the dog suggested to you by your seller. You will be surprised how much you can find out in this way, and you may well raise your eyebrows with excitement when you trace these details. Later, as you gain experience, you may consider adding a little of this and a little of that, in the nature of a mild outcross. But whatever you do, resist plunging in at the deep end. In the beginning you may be fired by ambition, but you will certainly lack experience, and this can be the downfall of many high hopes.

Another pitfall to avoid is the use of some local dog, just because he is handy. Employ instead the very best dog you can find for your bitch. The last thing you should be thinking about at this time is how much it will cost you. Also, consider very carefully before agreeing to any suggestions that a puppy should be given in lieu of a stud fee. You may find yourself parting with the 'flyer' of your litter, and if your bitch is a 'goose that lays golden eggs' and the dog is a proven sire of outstanding stock, the possibility of your being asked for a puppy could be much greater. It is always better to pay the stud fee and be done with it, because then you know where you are. You will, of course, come to an arrangement with the owner of the stud dog that in the event of the bitch not producing puppies — a somewhat rare occurrence in Staffordshire Bull Terriers — he will allow your bitch a free service on her next season. This is an unwritten law and I have never known a stud dog owner to quibble, because, naturally, he is as keen for his dog to sire something outstanding to your bitch as you are. However, it is as well to establish the point clearly when the first mating takes place.

I think we all agree that we need a masculine type of stud dog, one with substance. Remember that he cannot be expected to produce what he lacks himself, so do not listen to those who may tell you of the wonderful results produced by some little weed who was classically bred. Such a dog may sound very tempting, but take it from me and play safe. Choose a stud dog with an undeniable record and if his fee is a little higher than some others, do not let that influence you. If you feel he is the best one for your bitch, go for it! There is a great difference between investment and expense, and when you are using a stud dog's services you are making an investment. As well as substance, what else should you look for in a stud dog? Movement is one thing, and avoid using a stud dog who is poor in this area. Nine times out of ten, bad movers produce more bad movers. Never allow anyone to persuade you otherwise.

To sum it up, you need a stud dog who is strong and masculine, a good mover, as sound as a bell, and whose quarters and body are as near perfection as possible. What is more, his record should be able to speak for itself if he has been standing at stud for some time. On the other hand, you should not overlook the young dog, not yet much used, whose puppies are neither numerous or mature. A youngster whose breeding fits in with your programme in addition to his physical make-up is a distinct possibility.

Do not start negotiations for your stud dog when your bitch is just about ready for mating. Your mind should have been made up weeks previously and all the details settled long beforehand. People who own stud dogs like to have all their studs arranged well in advance, and if the dog has been booked to your bitch and all plans made, it is better to know the dog has not been used the day before, than to hope he has not when you arrive with your bitch. It might still be alright even if he has, but you don't want any *might* about it, you need to *know*. So, plan and book well ahead.

THE MATING

As soon as your bitch comes into season, contact the stud dog owner so you can arrange a date for the mating. This may have to be changed depending on how the season progresses, but at least the stud dog owner has an approximate date in mind. All animals are individuals and there is no hard and fast rule as to when a bitch will be ready for mating. The best course of action is to check your bitch daily, and be guided by the physical changes. When a bitch first comes in to season, she will pay great attention to her rear-end, constantly licking and cleaning herself. The first day of the season is counted from when you see a blood-coloured discharge. The vulva becomes increasingly swollen, and the bitch is usually ready for mating when the discharge becomes straw-coloured.

As a general guide, this usually happens between the twelfth and the fourteenth day of the season, but there have been many successful matings when the bitch has been mated earlier or later. It is a matter of reading the physical signs. If you have a male, you can soon find out if your bitch is receptive – as long as your are supervising proceedings. You can also test by stroking the bitch at her rear-end; if she is ready to stand, she will usually twitch her tail to one side.

It is customary to take the bitch to the stud dog for the mating. The stud dog owner will be in charge, but you will probably be called on to assist by holding your bitch at the crucial time. The dog and bitch will usually start off by playing and flirting together, and it will be quickly established whether the bitch is ready for mating. The male mounts the female, and the stud dog owner may assist by making sure the dog is in the correct position. After a few thrusts, the dog and bitch will be 'tied'. This is the period when the dog's swollen penis is held by the constricting muscles of the bitch's vagina. It is possible to have a successful mating without a tie, as the sperm can be passed in the initial thrusting. However, most breeders prefer to see a tie.

During the tie, the stud dog will usually dismount, and turn so that he is either standing side by side with the bitch, or rear-end to rear-end. The duration of the tie varies from five minutes to forty-five minutes – or more – but in most cases it will last around twenty minutes. When the dogs are separated, put your bitch back in the car, and do not allow her to urinate for an hour or so. In some cases, the stud dog owner will advise a second mating, and this should be no be more than forty-eight hours after the first, as it may cause problems with puppies being conceived at different times.

The stud fee is paid after the mating, and it is important to remember that you are paying for the service, regardless of the outcome. However, if your bitch fails to come into whelp, most stud dog owners will offer a free service the next time the bitch is in season. Make sure all your paperwork is completed, as this will be important when it comes to registering the puppies.

Chapter Twelve

PREGNANCY, WHELPING AND REARING

THE PREGNANCY

After your bitch has been mated, do not change her routine. All bitches handle pregnancy differently. Some show they are in whelp early, while others carry their puppies high in the ribs and do not show till they are about seven weeks in whelp. Start to give her more food after she is about six weeks pregnant, but not too much, as you want to avoid getting her too fat. Keep her exercise up, but on a lead. There should be no more free running for our pregnant mum.

If you take your bitch to your vet when she is about three weeks in whelp, he will more than likely be able to tell you whether she is pregnant. The puppies are just like golf balls at this stage and a vet can feel them. After four weeks the cycle changes, and they are not so easy to detect. My own way of telling when a bitch is pregnant is by checking her teats. They go a clear pink, the hair around them starts to recede and the nipples get larger.

Some bitches absorb their puppies at about five weeks. There can be many explanations for this distressing occurrence, but to suggest any individual reason would be mere conjecture. Happily, we do not see it too often in Staffordshire Bull Terriers. It is always advisable to worm your bitch before you mate her. As she progresses into the last weeks of her pregnancy, try not to give her too many drinks before you put her to bed for the night, since the pressure on her bladder becomes greater with the growth of the puppies inside her. If she has a little accident, don't scold her, because she is not her normal self and she will be more upset than you are.

At this stage, if you put your bitch quietly down on her side you will be able to see her puppies moving. The period of gestation is normally sixty-three days, but bitches can give birth a week before, or even a week after, this date. You should keep an eye on the mucus from her vagina. If it is clear, everything is normal.

THE WHELPING

We generally find that our bitches go off their food about twenty-four hours before they whelp, and, about a couple of hours before they have their first pup, they begin to dig up their bed and start to pant heavily. Try to keep your bitch in her whelping box because, if she gets the chance, she will have her puppies on your bed. Quietly reassure her, and all should be well. When the first contractions come, she will arch her back and push. The water bag will appear first, and by then the puppy will be in the birth canal and with another hefty push will be expelled. If she keeps pressing and nothing happens after half an hour, take her for a brisk walk up and down the garden. Just be careful that a puppy does not pop out as she sits down to relieve herself, and then take her back inside. If she does not have her first puppy within two hours after this, you must phone your vet, whom you should have warned at least two weeks previously.

You may have to take her to the surgery where the vet can have a closer look at her. Sometimes an injection of pituitrin is enough to start labour; if this does not do the trick, the vet may have to start thinking of a Caesarian section. This is very unusual for a Staffordshire Bull Terrier, but occasionally necessary. I hope you never have to experience this, as it normally takes twenty-four hours after the operation for the bitch to accept her puppies. Even after this you have to keep an eye on her for about three days, just in case she lies on her babies.

There is never a set pattern as to when each whelp will appear, but normally it is about every half hour. It can sometimes take longer than this, in fact I have known it to take 24 hours, but again this is very unusual. Having said that, no bitch should be left between pups for more than three hours, and if you suspect that she is in distress, contact your vet as soon as possible.

During the birth, if any of the puppies present the wrong way round (i.e. back feet first), I take a bit of clean towelling and get hold of the puppy by the back legs. When the bitch has her next contraction, I pull down and between the bitch's legs, the action being in the shape of a horseshoe. When your bitch has her first puppy, the afterbirth will come immediately afterwards. It is quite normal for the bitch to eat this, and in doing so, she will start to lick at her back end, thus starting the cycle again for the next puppy.

The first thing you should do after the bitch has cleaned up, is to make sure the puppy gets put on to the bitch's best teat. This is usually one of the back four. Press gently on the teat, just to get the colostrum flowing. It is very important for the puppy to have this substance, as it could keep it nourished for up to twenty-four hours, and will provide the immunisation that the puppy needs to protect it for at least eight weeks. As soon as the bitch has whelped and all the puppies are safely sucking, she should be given some warm milk and glucose. She could be offered cold milk (warm milk may make her sleepy) in between the arrivals of the puppies and, in the case of a large litter where the bitch is becoming exhausted, she could be offered the milk with half to one teaspoonful of brandy in it, according to her size.

EATING THE AFTERBIRTH

There is quite a difference of opinion as to whether or not the bitch should be permitted to eat the afterbirth, or placenta, from each puppy. Many vets do not recommend this. The placenta is very high in protein content and full of hormones, which have accumulated in it since conception. It also contains iron and oxygen. It is obvious, therefore, that the placenta must contain a great deal of nourishment, particularly proteins and iron. The hormones which have accumulated play a large part in stimulating the bitch's milk, and they also help the uterus to contract after a whelping is completed. I personally feel that bitches should be permitted to eat up to three afterbirths, should they wish to do so. What you have got to watch out for is that the bitch does not choke on a placenta, especially if she tries to swallow it whole. If the bitch eats too many afterbirths from a large litter, indigestion, colic and gastritis can occur, and they are extremely likely to induce diarrhoea in the bitch.

The new mother spends quite some time licking her rear-end in order to clean herself, and occasionally she may eat a placenta without the owner realising that she has done so. If the litter is large, placentas which are not eaten should be placed in a bowl or a small box, where they can be counted later. The number eaten by the bitch should also be counted, for if there is any doubt about whether an afterbirth has emerged, the vet should be informed. The bitch will probably be given an injection of pituitary extract, which will help her to expel any retained placentas. Sometimes a puppy may be retained, and this is even more dangerous. Unless both puppy and placenta are expelled within seventy-two hours, the bitch will probably die from acute infection.

The main argument against allowing bitches to eat the afterbirths is that they will be fed an adequate diet after they have whelped, and that there is therefore no need for extra nourishment. Moreover, the eating of the afterbirth is a relic from the days when dogs were wild and bitches had to eat all the afterbirths in order to hide the scent from dangerous animals who might become aware of the presence of the young. Most bitches like to eat the afterbirths and some seem to do so with much relish. While doing so, they will often take no notice of their puppies and will be thoroughly preoccupied.

Some bitches will swallow the afterbirth whole, while others spend some time chewing and gnawing it. Some may only eat part of a placenta, leaving the rest in a corner, and will bury it as if keeping it for a future occasion. If a bitch does not wish to eat the afterbirth, it is better to remove it. Most bitches can manage to eat four afterbirths without any inconvenience. The reason for this is probably that wild dogs and wolves normally have litters of only four or five puppies, and nature probably therefore intended the bitch to eat the same number of placentas. The domestication of the dog has produced many breeds which have extra-large litters, but canine digestive organs have not altered enough to be able to cope with too many afterbirths.

REMOVAL OF PUPPIES WHILE WHELPING

This very much depends on the individual bitch, how many puppies she is carrying, and how quickly they arrive. It also depends on whether she is whelping in a proper whelping box with a pig-rail, which is a rail attached all the way round the inside of the box, designed to stop the bitch rolling on to her pups. It is usually best to leave the first puppy with the dam until the arrival of the second one. If the bitch is very restless, turning around frequently, and scratching her box, then it is probably safer to remove the puppy and place it on a warm blanket on a warm hot-water bottle, or better still, in a small box under an infra-red lamp, close at hand to the bitch. As soon as the bitch has settled down after the arrival of each puppy, all the puppies should be returned to her, because they require stimulation from the licking of her tongue and from sucking. If the puppies are left alone, they will not move and will just drop off to sleep, and this is not good for them.

Some bitches become very agitated if the puppies are removed. If the litter is large, it is perhaps a good idea to let her keep one or two puppies, so that she may not miss the rest. If she becomes unduly worried or distressed, then provided she has a whelping box with a pig-rail, she may be allowed to keep all her puppies. It is really a matter of discretion and observation as to whether all the puppies should be removed, or just some of them, or none. Some owners remove pups only when another is actually being delivered. On the whole, it is far better to allow a bitch to do everything she can for her puppies on her own.

THE NEWBORN PUPPY

As soon as a puppy is born, it is essential that the membranes should be removed immediately, either by the dam or by her human helper, in order to enable the newcomer to breathe. The puppy generally gives one or two gasps, but it often has difficulty in starting to breathe. At first a puppy's breathing is shallow and rather weak, but after a very short time, it usually becomes quite normal. It is always a bad sign if the puppy breathes with its mouth open. Some puppies are born looking as if they are quite dead, with no movement and no signs of respiration. It is essential to start a puppy breathing immediately. As soon as it is breathing properly, it will quite vigorously crawl towards the dam's teats and will quickly find one and start sucking. If there are already several other puppies, it may be necessary to put the newest one to a back teat.

The first milk from the teat contains a mild laxative, and it is important that the puppies should get it into their intestines as soon as possible. This stimulates an action within the puppy's bowels and ensures that their contents are expelled. The first evacuation is called by its medical name

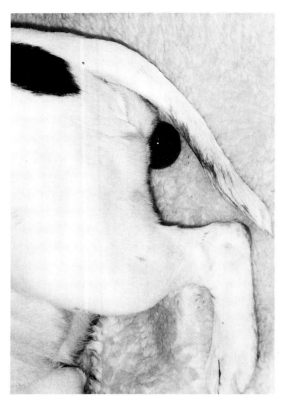

The bag showing at the bitch's vulva is known as the water bag. When this bursts the bitch will start to have strong contractions. The vulva will start to swell and she will push her tail up high as the puppy is pushed out.

The mother licks the membrane from her newborn puppy. This stimulates the puppy to give a large gasp and fill its lungs with air.

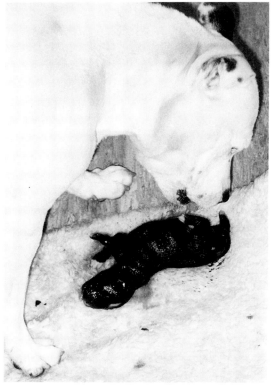

'meconium' – a black, gummy substance which accumulates in the bowel prior to birth. It consists partly of the debris from mucous membranes lining the intestines, and partly of bile which has been secreted by the liver. It is important that the puppy should pass meconium as early as possible, because until this occurs, proper digestion cannot take place. Colostrum, which is the dam's first milk, also acts as a mild purgative. The puppy is stimulated to evacuate the bowels by the licking of the bitch's tongue. In the case of a weak puppy, the helper should try to get it to pass the meconium by gently stimulating it with a small piece of moistened cotton wool, gently stroking the abdomen. Normally, the puppies have no difficulty in evacuating meconium.

A GUIDE TO NORMAL WHELPING

1. A drop in the bitch's temperature 24-48 hours prior to whelping.
2. The bitch lies stretched out with her head between her forelegs.
3. She becomes progressively more and more restless — a sure sign that labour has started.
4. She looks at and licks her rear parts.
5. She refuses food (though this is not always the case).
6. She is occasionally sick.
7. The vulva is swollen and soft, with a clear mucous discharge.
8. She starts to push and strain in the second stage of labour.
9. You should time the bitch's progress from this stage.
10. She generally starts tearing the bedding in between pains, and pants.
11. Intermittent regular or irregular pains continue from one to three hours, sometimes longer. If longer than three hours, call the vet.
12. Appearance of the water bag. This must not be mistaken for a puppy.
13. The bag generally breaks of its own accord, or is broken by the bitch.
14. The puppy appears soon after this, nose first with the forelegs facing forward and tucked under the chin.
15. The puppy is born. Break the membrane by the nose.
16. Draw out the placenta, if it is not expelled by a contraction.
17. Sever the cord by pinching and tearing.
18. Dry the puppy and put it on to a teat to suck.
19. The bitch will probably eat the afterbirth.
20. Weigh the puppy.
21. Clean up any mess, and place clean paper in the box.
22. Feed the bitch with some cold milk and glucose, if necessary adding brandy.
23. Allow the bitch to rest after the birth of each puppy.
24. Let the bitch out for a while to relieve herself, if whelping is protracted.
25. Make sure that all placentas are accounted for, particularly the final one, and that there are no more puppies. If in doubt, call your vet.
26. Danger signs: strong contractions over a period of two hours with no visible result; the cessation of contractions for several hours; collapse of the bitch, or signs of twitching. In the unlikely event of contractions being resumed after a long interval, they are generally not strong enough to expel more than one puppy.

CARE OF THE LITTER

Every stage of a dog's life is exciting, but the most thrilling is when the little 'time-wasters' have arrived. I call them that because, along with most people, I suppose, puppies cause me to spend so much time watching them and playing with them when I know full well I should be doing some other job around the kennels. Still, I love my baby Staffords and am sure you do too. So, let's keep doing it!

You should bear in mind that puppies may be born with worms or may pick up eggs immediately after birth. If they are badly infected, they should be wormed as early as five weeks of age, for such puppies stand a very good chance of succumbing to their first serious illness. If you are concerned about them, consult your vet; he will provide you with some of the excellent worming tablets that are on the market today. You can have your puppies vaccinated as early as eight weeks of age, again at twelve weeks, and then again at sixteen weeks. Never delay it at twelve weeks, as the puppy needs the protection of a vaccine that will last until at least sixteen weeks, when full inoculations can be given. You must not let your new puppy out of the precincts of your garden. If you live in a flat, you must train the pup to use newspaper until it is old enough to be immunised.

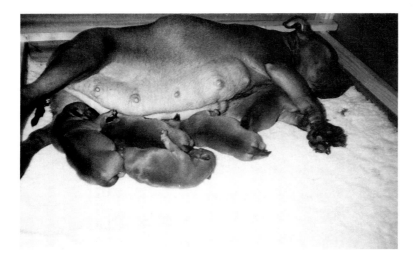

In the first week of life, the puppies do little more than eat and sleep, and their mother provides for all their needs.

This red puppy is two weeks old. Note how dark the coat is; this will turn to a deep red by the time the puppy is six weeks old. The shading between the stop and the back of the skull indicates what colour the coat will be in maturity.

At three weeks of age, this litter is evenly matched and has obviously enjoyed the benefits of good rearing.

The sire of the litter is often forgotten after the litter has been born, but Finnish Ch. Gallant Quiet Man is taking a keen interest in his son.

When the time for weaning comes, the change from mother's milk to a solid diet and other milk foods must not be abrupt. From the age of three to four weeks, puppies can be taught to take a little scraped fresh lean raw meat. At first, you may find it necessary to get them to do this by offering it on the finger. They will start by sucking it off rather than chewing it, but they will soon learn; the most important thing is to get them to take it in the first place, which they usually do without any difficulty. They should be taught to lap milky food and so on. Gradually increase the amount of meat daily, and they will soon get into the swing of things.

There is little danger of puppies overeating at this stage, although common sense plays its part. Cod-liver oil may be given in small quantities twice a week from the beginning of weaning. After the puppies have got over the initial weaning and are on to solid food proper, they should be fed five times a day until they are ten or twelve weeks old. Always remember in winter that if the last

Puppies go through periods of intense activity when they explore their surroundings.

At ten weeks of age, this brindle and white puppy is showing good all-round development.

Playtimes are alternated with long periods of sleep, which are equally important for the growing puppy.

Every breeder aspires to produce a show-quality litter, but this should never become more important than rearing sound dogs of good temperament.

feed is given at, say, 6pm owing to the long winter night, it is far too long for them to go without food until about 8am the following day. Bear this in mind and feed, if you can possibly manage it, the last meal of the day quite late at night. We like our puppies to have their last feed about ten or eleven o'clock at night. They are then fed quite early next morning. If you keep to this routine, your puppies will not fall back in any way. Always remember the golden rule, feed little and often, rather than fewer heavier meals. Excessive pot-bellies in pups can cause weak hocks and loose shoulders. So let the puppies stuff themselves with a number of smaller meals, for they need all the body-building food and nourishment they can get. Through the months of puppyhood you can see your litter growing before your eyes. If they are properly fed, they will look strong and healthy, and a well-nourished puppy is a joy to behold.

Chapter Thirteen

WHELPING COMPLICATIONS

ABSORPTION OF WHELPS

All bitches mated at the right time, unless they are infertile, will conceive, but sometimes all or some of the puppies become absorbed. Bitches seldom abort a puppy. The whelps are normally absorbed and do not seem to go septic. Occasionally, when a large litter is born naturally, a partly-formed whelp will arrive. This is one which has developed normally until a certain stage, after which, perhaps owing to there being too many whelps, it did not receive sufficient nourishment. Possibly what happens is that the placentas get pushed together and one becomes separated. When these whelps are expelled, they have no odour and are often split when born or resemble jelly babies. In early pregnancy, the whelps can be completely absorbed and cause no trouble. Sometimes they become mummified, and these are generally only discovered during a Caesarian section, or an elderly bitch may develop a lump which turns out to be an ossified whelp. Very occasionally, one of these mummified whelps will be passed normally.

UTERINE INERTIA

In Staffords, we do not normally see this problem, but it can happen when the litter is small and the puppies large. The bitch will strain fruitlessly for too long a period, and her uterus will become exhausted until finally there are no more contractions. There is another cause of inertia, which is possibly hereditary and results from a hormonal imbalance, which causes the contractions to be weak and finally cease altogether. If you ever have the misfortune to encounter this, never buy or keep a puppy from such a mating, nor should the bitch be bred from again.

The main concern for the bitch with this problem during the birth is to help her by means of injections of callo-Cal-D, which can be given intramuscularly. Generally, after a period of about twenty minutes, contractions will start again. If they are weak, a further injection may be given. Provided the birth canal is fully dilated, injections of pituitary extract can be administered intramuscularly. This is a very powerful drug, and should only be given by the veterinary surgeon or under his supervision. Injection of this drug before the birth canal is fully dilated, or in too high doses, can cause very serious complications. The bitch will generally start having contractions again between five and twenty minutes after an injection, and the puppies are often then born quite easily, though occasionally the bitch may require further injections. If, however, no further progress is being made, then the vet will normally perform a Caesarian section.

In severe cases of uterine inertia the whelps cannot be born without an injection of pituitary extract for each whelp. If the uterus has been contracting so strongly that it has become exhausted, then even pituitary extract is useless. A warning against this wonderful but exceedingly powerful drug is that it can cause a ruptured or inverted uterus. However, provided that the breeder uses common sense and that no bitch is permitted to continue straining for longer than two or, at the very most three, hours of fruitless contractions, this mishap should never occur.

COMPLETE INERTIA

Sometimes the water bag (amniotic sac) breaks, and the only indication that this has happened may be the evidence of damp bedding. The bitch sometimes tears up paper, makes a nest, and will even start panting, but she never gets as far as visible contractions. This may sometimes occur after a previous Caesarian section, owing to the possibility of adhesions. If the bitch does not go into a normal labour within a short time, the vet must be informed, and you should not delay getting assistance for more than two or three hours after the bag has burst. Assistance must be sought even if the bag breaks at night. The bitch should not be permitted to go unattended, as there is a strong possibility that the whelps may die, and even a possibility of losing the bitch.

MANUAL MANIPULATION

Sometimes a puppy can be seen at the vulva, but there is no progress with the expulsion. To assist in extracting the puppy, which must be done under aseptic conditions, the nails of the manipulator should be short and free from jagged edges. Women with very long, thin fingers can generally manipulate a puppy more easily than men who have large hands and fat fingers. The hands should be thoroughly washed and some antiseptic cream applied. A finger should then be inserted very gently into the vagina, so that it can be hooked round the puppy, preferably over the back of its neck. Then, as the bitch strains, gently but steadily pull the puppy downwards and outwards. This will often give the bitch just that little extra help she requires, particularly when she is tired and it is a first puppy, which is so often the largest, or with one of the last arrivals in a large litter, when the bitch may be getting exhausted. It is always better in difficult cases to get your vet's assistance, but sometimes this may be delayed an hour or so, and then it is better to help the bitch as much as possible under such circumstances.

DIFFICULT HEAD PRESENTATION

In cases where the head is born and the back is uppermost, but the puppy does not arrive within a few seconds, the membranes should be torn apart at the mouth, so that the puppy can breathe a little, despite its lungs being constricted. It is best to grasp the puppy at the top of the neck just below its head between the first two fingers and, as the bitch strains, to pull the head downwards and forwards and between her hind legs towards her nose, keeping a steady traction. If the puppy does not come away immediately and there is difficulty with the shoulders, gently pull the head to one side and then the other. This should release the shoulders. If there is a limb or foot protruding, pull that leg forward and outwards towards the bitch's tail. This should release one shoulder from the pelvic brim and the same should then be done with the other limb.

Once the wedge-shaped shoulders are through the pelvic brim, the puppy should not be drawn out towards the bitch's tail, but round and forward as I have just explained. The shoulders often act as a wedge in the brim of the pelvis, so it is essential to release one shoulder at a time. As soon as the shoulders are free of the brim, a slight corkscrew action will often help to deliver a tight-fitting puppy. Sometimes, if the whelp is large and the shoulders are out, it is a good idea to change the grip. Taking a small cloth or a large piece of cotton wool, grip the puppy firmly by the whole extruding part and continue pulling, with a gentle but firm traction. The head and shoulders are the heaviest part of the puppy, so that if they come first, the centre of gravity is forward and this aids the uterine contractions to expel the puppy more quickly.

BREECH PRESENTATION

If it is found that the tail and hind legs are presented and the water bag is intact, the feet should be grasped when they are first sighted and held firmly, so that they do not disappear back into the bitch. In breech presentations, particularly with a large pup, or if the bag has broken, every second counts. The feet are very slippery, and it is very easy for you to lose your grip. If the feet go up into the bitch again, it may be a few valuable minutes before they appear once more, and in this time, if the bag has broken or the placenta has started to come away from the uterus, the puppy is likely to drown or to be asphyxiated. It is always easier to hold any part of a puppy which has been extruded in some form of cloth, or even a wad of cotton-wool. Great care must be taken not to pinch the feet: it is essential that the traction should be gentle but firm. It has been known for an over-enthusiastic helper to actually pull the feet off a pup, and so, obviously, great care must be taken.

Keep a steady traction on the feet and, regardless of whether the bitch is straining or not, try to pull the puppy out by steady, gentle, but strong traction, because, unless the puppy is born within a minute or two, it will be dead. If the position is bad and the puppy has been held up for a long time in the pelvic brim, the blood supply from the cord itself gets cut off and the puppy then has neither oxygen nor its blood supply from the dam. Should the placenta have started to separate from the uterine wall at this stage, then both oxygen and blood supply will be denied to the puppy and, unless it is extracted quickly, it will die.

All books I have read on the subject invariably say that on no account should a puppy be pulled out unless there is a contraction. This, of course, is essential in the case of a human birth, because the vulva and vagina are both easily torn. In the case of dogs, however, I have many times had to pull a puppy out without a contraction, in order to save its life, and I have never known the vulva to tear. Whelps are remarkably strong and can stand quite a strong traction, but it is essential that it should be slow, steady and in the right direction, which is downwards and towards the bitch's nose. In the case of a feet-first puppy, there is really no alternative in order to save it. It is also better for the bitch to have one bad pain with its removal, than to wear herself out, straining fruitlessly to expel a dead puppy.

In general, it is reasonably easy to get a breech puppy out as far as the shoulders, it should then be pulled slightly to one side to release one shoulder and when that is through the brim, the puppy should be pulled in the opposite direction to release the other shoulder. Unfortunately, when the puppy has been expelled thus far, there is often difficulty in getting the head out. If a puppy is expected to be large, a little liquid paraffin should be syringed into the vagina when the feet appear, particularly if the water bag has broken. This helps lubricate the passage. The difficulty with the head in these cases is not necessarily the disparity in size between the bitch and the puppy's head, but is more likely to be that the birth passage is not completely dilated. In any case, if there is any chance that the puppy may survive, then it must be removed immediately.

If the breech is arriving with difficulty, it can be a great help for someone to stand the bitch on her feet and to hold her abdomen up, so that the puppy inside her is supported on the hand, while the second person takes hold of whatever part of the puppy is protruding, often the hind feet. Keep a strong, steady traction on the feet, and, as more of the puppy emerges and without letting go of what has already appeared, take hold with the other hand of the next part of the puppy. Gradually draw the puppy downwards and forwards. It is easier to do this if the puppy is grasped in a cloth, because it is very slippery. If the puppy gets stuck at the shoulders, pull first to one side to free one shoulder and then to the other side to free the other, or a slight corkscrew movement will probably help to get the shoulder out. Having got this far, it is often found that there is difficulty in getting the head out, particularly in the case of a large puppy. It helps to a certain extent, if the bitch is still standing at this stage, to pull the pup's body right down so that the abdomen of the puppy is nearly against the abdomen of the bitch. Puppies which have had such a difficult birth will probably need reviving with brandy and artificial respiration.

RETENTION OF THE AFTERBIRTH
This is not an uncommon occurrence, particularly if the bitch has not been watched carefully. It is generally the last placenta which gets left in the horn of the uterus. If there is any doubt whether any of the placentas may have been retained, particularly the last one, the vet should examine the bitch, and will generally administer an injection of pituitary extract, which makes the uterus contract and expel the retained afterbirth. Most vets give some form of antibiotic as a precaution against infection, which could cause septicaemia and would be highly dangerous for the bitch.

RETAINED PUPPY
After a bitch has whelped, it is often extraordinarily difficult to be completely certain that there is not still another puppy to come. Immediately after the birth of a puppy, if there is another puppy in the horn of the uterus, it is usually possible to feel it by palpating the abdomen with both hands, but if the bitch is not felt immediately, the uterus seems to fill up and becomes soft. It is then very difficult to be certain whether there is really a puppy there or not. Much later the uterus contracts in size and may then often be mistaken for another puppy.

So difficult is it to tell, that it has been known for a bitch to have whelped six or seven puppies and yet be thought to have a retained puppy, upon which a Caesarian section has been performed, only to find nothing. This is an extremely dangerous situation for a bitch, to have undergone whelping a large litter and then to have such a serious operation. The extreme danger to the bitch, however, of having a retained puppy must also be fully appreciated. Sometimes, a bitch may be perfectly healthy after whelping with no abnormally high temperature, but when she is put out to relieve herself, she may start straining as if she were constipated, and if she continues to do so, she probably has a retained puppy. It is then absolutely imperative that your vet's assistance should be obtained immediately. A pituitary extract injection will probably be given, but unless this produces the puppy rapidly, a Caesarian section will be necessary.

A retained puppy is a great source of infection, particularly if it has been dead for more than twenty-four hours. The longer a puppy is retained, the more ill the bitch will become and the higher her temperature. A retained placenta can give similar symptoms and can be equally dangerous. After the removal of the retained puppy or placenta the bitch will be seriously ill. The puppies will have to be hand-reared until the bitch's temperature is normal. Provided the bitch has adequate supervision, and, if in doubt whether there is a retained puppy or placenta, a pituitary extract injection is given, and provided that the bitch is under the surveillance of a vet, the tragedy of losing her should never occur. There are many recorded cases in which bitches have produced calcified puppies or parts of puppies up to six weeks after they should have been born. The bitches in these cases are seriously ill and many have to be put to sleep. It cannot be stressed too strongly, therefore, how important is proper observation of the bitch after whelping.

RESUSCITATION OF A PUPPY
Most puppies come into the world, take one or two small gasps, then start to cry, and from then on breathe normally. There are, however, a number of puppies who arrive and look to all intents and purposes as if they were dead. Puppies may arrive with varying degrees of difficulty in breathing, and this depends largely on the complications of their birth, and whether labour has been unduly prolonged. As we have seen, problems can also occur if for some reason the placenta becomes

prematurely separated from the uterus, in which case the oxygen supply is cut off from the puppy. Some puppies arrive in a very flaccid state. They seem to be twice as long as they should be, and consequently are thin and flat, making no movement after they are born. Provided that quick treatment is given, they sometimes survive.

Regardless of how a puppy is born or even if it is breathing normally and crying, it should be lifted up with its neck well supported and given a sharp shake downwards in order to dislodge any mucus or fluid which may have been sucked into its air passages. The mouth should be opened, and the very act of doing this may cause it to give a gasp. If the puppy is not breathing, or if it is breathing badly or with difficulty, its tongue should be pulled forward, and a drop of brandy can be placed on the back of the tongue. The pup can also be given a whiff of weak smelling salts, which will cause the puppy to take a breath, and possibly shake its head and even wrinkle its nose with distaste or give a tiny squeal.

Stimulate the puppy by rubbing the hair on the nape of its neck the wrong way. You can hold the puppy in the palms of both hands, with its head in the right hand, its feet in the left, and its tummy facing downwards. Quite forcibly, bring the knuckles together, making the puppy concave, then reverse the procedure, so that the puppy's back is slightly convex. Bringing the knuckles together and separating them in this way about twenty times to the minute will often stimulate a puppy which is not breathing well to start doing so normally. After five minutes, another drop of brandy could be placed on its tongue and smelling salts applied again. Squeezing the rib cage every second or half second will also help to stimulate the heart, and start it beating normally. This often stimulates a puppy to breathe too. If the air passages remain blocked, cover the puppy's nose and mouth with your mouth, keeping your head bent back and the puppy's head down, suck hard and spit out the slightly sweet fluid. The puppy must be stimulated sufficiently in order to make it take a deep enough breath to help its heart to start beating properly, and there is often no more trouble, once breathing has been established.

The novice must be warned that it is dangerous to give strong smelling salts to very small puppies, because they can have the opposite effect of over-stimulation. Smelling salts should not, therefore, be offered too frequently. Another method of reviving a puppy is to rub it quite vigorously in a hot towel. Also try holding it in both hands and, starting above your head, swinging your arms down between your legs. This sounds rather drastic, but it will often stimulate a puppy sufficiently to start normal breathing. Great care must be taken when doing this, because it has been known for a puppy to slide right out of someone's hands on to the floor. Yet another method is for the puppy to be tipped first on to its head, so that the contents of the abdomen fall on to its lungs and depress them. The puppy is then tipped up on to its hind legs, so that the contents of the abdomen drop back again. This first causes a vacuum in the lungs which, when released, sucks air into them. This, again, can be continued about twenty times a minute.

PROBLEMS WITH THE PLACENTA

Occasionally, there is a very short umbilical cord, or the cord breaks before the placenta has been expelled. Do not worry unduly about this: as the bitch starts to bear down for the delivery of her next puppy, the first afterbirth will be expelled.

If it is not, ignore it for a while, as the most important thing is to make sure that everything is all right with the puppy. It is, however, always wise to count the afterbirths when you get the chance. The exception to the easy expulsion of all the membranes is frequently the placenta belonging to the last puppy born. This puppy probably occupied the extremity of one of the horns of the uterus. If, by chance, the placenta is retained in the uterus, it will cause either a mild or a severe metritis, which is an inflammation of the uterus, until the foreign body is expelled. In the case of complete retention the results could be exceedingly serious, as we have seen above.

CAESARIAN SECTION

This is the removal of the unborn puppy from the dam by surgical operation. These days, now that anaesthetics have so greatly improved, there is very little risk of the bitch not surviving, provided that she has not been permitted to undergo a long and arduous labour. It is not unknown for a bitch to go into shock as soon as the anaesthetic is administered, just before the end of the operation, or soon after. On the whole, however, Caesarian section is reasonably safe and far better than allowing a bitch to strain fruitlessly without result.

There are various causes which make a section a necessity. It is generally performed because of an abnormally large puppy, or a whelp in a bad position. Occasionally, it may be performed owing to a deformed pelvis in the bitch, and it needs to be performed in some cases of uterine inertia, which may occur in varying degrees. In a protracted labour, or where labour ceases altogether, a Caesarian section is absolutely essential in order to save the bitch.

Most bitches come round a few minutes after the last stitch has been inserted. The bitch should be kept reasonably warm in a clean box, and it is better to have the puppies in another box, until she has completely recovered from the anaesthetic, because until she is quite conscious, the bitch may stumble around, turn about and accidentally lie on a puppy and kill it. The chief dangers after a Caesarian section are haemorrhage and shock. There is also the possibility of sepsis, but with modern antibiotic injections this seldom occurs. Puppies may possibly have difficulty in breathing after they have been delivered, as they will have taken a certain amount of the anaesthetic into their bloodstreams from the dam. These puppies should never be given up for dead too soon. We always try to revive our puppies by wrapping each one in a towel with its head pointing downwards, and with both hands grasping the body we sway the puppy between our knees. This seems to bring them round quicker and they then cry normally.

It is a good idea to save at least one placenta after the operation to rub over the puppies, because, as soon as the bitch has come round properly, she will accept her puppies more readily if she can smell the placenta on them. As soon as the bitch is conscious, she should be handed one puppy at a time to lick before it is placed on a teat. This should be done to each puppy in turn, and the bitch should be carefully watched to make quite certain that she has accepted the puppies, particularly if it is her first litter.

Luckily, bitches who have a Caesarian section suffer from no psychological problems as humans sometimes do. It can be a great shock for a bitch to wake up and find herself surrounded with a number of squeaking, squirming puppies. It is not surprising if at first she does not quite understand where they came from or how they got there, but with a little encouragement most bitches settle down quickly with their puppies. There are some breeds who will never accept their puppies after a Caesarian, but fortunately, we don't see this problem in Staffordshire Bull Terriers. The more the puppies suck, the quicker the uterus will contract, and this is very important.

The bitch should be kept on a light diet. When she is let out to relieve herself, it is quite extraordinary how she will have no idea that she has stitches in her abdomen and, unless prevented, she is quite likely to run at full speed even up stairs, to get back to her puppies. This could be highly dangerous, of course, as the wound will not have healed and a stitch could break. The bitch must, therefore, not be permitted to walk more than necessary and certainly not to jump. The wound heals surprisingly quickly and often leaves no scar, and the stitches are generally removed about the ninth or tenth day. The wound should be checked daily to ensure that all is well. Occasionally, there may be a swelling around the edge of a stitch, but this is generally not important unless it is inflamed, in which case veterinary assistance is required immediately.

Bitches are usually very good about allowing their puppies to feed from them after the operation, although this must make the area extremely sore and tender. If a litter is large, the puppies should have their dam's milk supplemented for a few days, to enable the bitch to regain her strength. A Caesarian section in no way affects the bitch as a brood bitch, because she may well whelp quite normally the next time she is mated, but it would be wise to allow her to miss her next season without mating her. Furthermore, it is not really advisable to let a bitch have more than two Caesarians, as each operation produces some adhesions. Sections are best avoided and certainly those caused by improper care should never happen. Some bitches may not be exercised adequately, or may be over-fed on unsuitable foods and consequently become too fat. A combination of such factors is hardly likely to induce a normal, satisfactory whelping.

POST-WHELPING COMPLICATIONS

ECLAMPSIA

One of the most common complications after whelping is eclampsia. This is due to a fall in the level of the blood calcium, whose causes are not exactly known. It is probably due to a calcium-controlled mechanism which is extremely complex and involves all the internal secreting glands, and may be caused by over-activity of the pituitary gland. This in turn secretes hormones, so that the delicate balance required for the control of calcium is upset and the level in the blood falls. It is interesting that this never occurs among wild animals, whereas animals that are in good condition and well-fed, but who receive only minimal amounts of exercise, are often the ones who suffer from this imbalance of calcium.

Eclampsia is sometimes called 'milk-fever', as it occasionally occurs a few hours before whelping and sometimes within three days after whelping. It also commonly occurs at about the third or fourth week after whelping. The cases which occur at this time are generally milder than the early cases, but they often take longer to recover from. It is said that eclampsia is more common after an easy whelping than after a difficult one, but this does not mean that bitches who have a difficult whelping cannot develop eclampsia. Latest research advises doses of Vitamin D, which enables the body to increase the absorption of calcium and phosphorus. If a blood sample is taken at the time of eclampsia, there will be a shortage of calcium in the blood. There is often too little phosphorus and possibly a lack of magnesium too. To avoid cases of eclampsia in the whelping bitch, therefore, it is necessary to give her some form of calcium with Vitamin D.

The symptoms of eclampsia start with general restlessness and nervousness, and an air of discomfort and apprehension. The temperature will be sub-normal and the bitch may vomit. As soon as this is noticed, the vet should be sent for so that large quantities of calcium burogluconate solution may be injected immediately. If this is not done, the bitch will grow progressively worse, start frothing at the mouth and eventually go into convulsions. Another early symptom is stiffness of the hind legs, and this continues into convulsions with jerky movements. Eventually the bitch may become rigid. Only in very severe cases is consciousness completely lost, but, provided that large doses of calcium are injected, the bitch will generally recover. Bitches may suffer from eclampsia at the end of lactation, when they have nursed a large litter. This gives rise to another name for this trouble, which is 'nursing fits'. It is, therefore, extremely important to observe all bitches a week before they whelp and particularly after they have whelped, and to continue to observe them until they have finished weaning their puppies.

If the calcium deficiency is treated immediately after the early symptoms of eclampsia are noticed and before convulsions start, the owner will have a great sense of achievement in having saved the bitch's life. Convulsions are caused by a condition in the brain, which has probably been set up by an irritation in the uterus. I, personally, have had eclampsia in my bitches – not one of my Staffords, but a Bull Terrier. For some unknown reason Bull Terriers seem to suffer far more from this condition than any breed I know. You should talk to your vet and ask advice about having a calcium injection, which is a very good way of assisting the bitch with a calcium booster before she starts lactating.

MASTITIS

This is inflammation of a milk gland. It occurs in bitches with an excess quantity of milk. The milk accumulates in a gland, either because there are not enough puppies, or because the puppies suck from other teats, or are too weak to suck properly. A teat is often ignored because there is more milk in the other teats and it is easier to obtain, so the puppies naturally make for those teats.

Mastitis may also be caused by a bacterial infection. The vet must treat the condition, usually with antibiotics, and drug treatment will alleviate the pain. Mastitis can often be prevented if the bitch is examined daily, and any teat which looks congested should have a puppy placed on it in order to draw the milk before it becomes stale. In more serious cases, the gland can be massaged gently with olive oil and the milk carefully drawn off. The teat should be back to normal within twenty-four hours. Some bitches' teats are flat, too small or too large for their puppies, and in such cases problems may occur.

Chapter Fourteen

THE STAFFORD WORLDWIDE

Breeders of Staffordshire Bull Terriers are constantly striving to improve the breed, and this has been a vital part in the development of the breed worldwide As the Stafford increases in popularity, it is essential to maintain quality and type so that the breed retains its umistakable identity, in terms of both appearance and temperament. We are fortunate to have many dedicated breeders who have the well-being of the Stafford at heart, and they have made a significant contribution to the breed.

UNITED KINGDOM

SENKRAH

The Senkrah kennel of Abe Harkness began in 1947 with his purchase of a brindle dog and bitch from Archie Renwick of Hamilton. Abe had some success with these two, but it was not until he bought two bitches from Mr George Down that he started to do really well. These bitches went by the names of Ch. Weycombe Julie and Ch. Weycombe Melody of Senkrah.

Ch. Weycombe Julie was mated to Ch. Eastaff Danom and from the mating came Ch. Sahib of Senkrah, winner of 17 CCs. He was the first Champion Stafford dog to be bred in Scotland. Ch. Weycombe Melody of Senkrah was also mated to Ch. Eastaff Danom twice without success. She was next mated to a local dog called MacGregor of Fauld, and this did the trick, producing seven excellent puppies. Of these, Saracen was the most notable for his reproduction of Champion stock. Abe had bought a bitch puppy to keep Melody company. She was called Senkrah Sabelle, and, although not top-class show quality, she was well bred. Abe thought she could produce something nice, but little did he know that this bitch would be the 'jewel in the crown' of his kennel.

When mated to Rex Underwood's dog, Weycombe Dandy, who was later to become Ch. Weycombe Dandy under his new ownership of Bruce and Eileen Nicholls, Sabelle produced from one litter Ch. Senkrah Saffron, Ch. Senkrah Sapphire, and the first International Champion of the breed, Senkrah Sabeau, owned by Raymond McEvoy. In her second litter, again to Ch. Weycombe Dandy, she produced Ch. Senkrah Sabutae, who was owned by Jack and Terry Miller, owners of the Rellim Kennels. Sabutae was the mother of Mr Derek Downs' Ch. Rellim Warpaint. Int. Ch. Senkrah Sabeau was the mother of the Hills' Ch. Kinderlee Cashelle. Ch. Weycombe Melody of Senkrah's son, Saracen of Senkrah, was the sire of two sisters, Ch. Sanville Wild Puma and Ch. Sanville Wild Cheetah. In fact, Saracen's breeding is behind all of the seven Sanville champions.

Abe's favourite stud dog, Senkrah Sabre, was a great influence in his breeding programme, and the likes of Ch. Anjemag Aussie, Ch. Sanville Red Rhapsody and Ch. Sanville Red Ember are just a few that this great dog was directly behind. At the time of writing, Abe is not breeding with the same enthusiasm as he has done in the past, and if we are not careful, we could easily lose this great kennel's bloodlines.

RELLIM

This kennel, owned by Jack Miller, was founded over forty years ago in partnership with his wife, Terry. Their foundation bitch was Ch. Wychbury Midly Girl (Queenie), who was acquired from Gerald Dudley's famous Wychbury kennel. A mating was planned between Queenie and her half-brother Ch. Wychbury Red Riband, but Jack and Terry had to wait for a repeat mating before Ch. Rellim Aboy, born 1957, was produced. This dog was considered to be an excellent specimen, although he was inclined to be aggressive in the show ring. He was used sparingly at stud, but a mating to the Irish bitch, Fury of Dugrade, produced the line which resulted in Ken Bailey's Ch. Benext Beau, who holds the record number of CCs in the breed. He also sired Ch. Rellim Ferryvale Victor, who went on to sire five English champions and many overseas Champions.

A bitch puppy was acquired from Abe Harkness's kennel, and Ch. Senkrah Sabuteau (Tammy) gained her title in just two years. Tammy was mated to Victor and the result was Ch. Rellim Warpaint and two bitches who went on to produce Champion stock. A young bitch by Warpaint was mated to Victor, and this produced Ch. Rellim Saratoga Skiddy – the first home-bred bitch. At about this time Rellim Cracklin Rose was produced, and she became a Champion in her new home in the USA. Other exports from the kennel included Can. Ch. Rellim Battle of Britain, Can. Ch. Rellim Kate of Terco and Am. Ch. Brother Love.

In 1975 Terry died at the tragically early age of forty-three, and since then Jack has continued the kennel on a very limited basis. The last litter (1985) produced Ch. Rellim Black Ace and Am. Ch. Rellim Task Force. Jack has been instrumental in developing the North East Staffordshire Bull Terrier Club, and has been made its Life President. This kennel's record of producing eight UK Champions and four overseas Champions has made a significant contribution to the breed.

EASTAFF

This kennel is owned by Joyce Shorrocks, and I personally think that she is one of the most talented of all our Staffordshire Bull Terrier breeders. Over the years, Joyce has continually produced the goods. In all, she has owned nine Champions, seven of which she bred herself.

Joyce started in Staffords in 1950. She purchased her first bitch from Jack McNeil in 1951, and this lovely bitch went on to become Ch. Linda of Killyglen. Joyce had lots of success with Linda, who produced three litters, including the great stud dog, Ch. Eastaff Danon. His sire was the beautifully line-bred dog Ch. Goldwyne Leading Lad. Ch. Eastaff Danon was in turn the sire of eleven English Champions, two Irish Champions and a South African Champion, a record that still stands to this day. Other Champions from Joyce were Ch. Eastaff Nicola, Ch. Eastaff Ironsides, Ch. Eastaff Noire Fille, Ch. Eastaff Lil' Stotter, and Ch. Eastaff Guardian who, if he had not met such an untimely death, would in my opinion have been a great stud dog. The other two English Champions were Ch. Constones Eastaff This'll Do, and a dog that I had a great liking for, Ch. Teutonic Warrior. I gave him his first Challenge Certificate, when he was still under eighteen months and was handled by a very young Master Rivenberg, in partnership with whom Joyce owned the dog. Ch. Teutonic Warrior was the top stud dog in the UK in 1986, and is behind most of the top reds in the UK at the moment.

Mrs Shorrocks is also a Championship Show judge of international repute, having judged in Finland, Germany, the United States of America and South Africa. She has graced many a dog show ring in the United Kingdom with her forthright approach to judging, which is so highly sought after.

Ch. Eastaff Guardian: Tragically, this dog died young before he could make his mark on the breed.

JACKSTAFF

Steve Halifax's Jackstaff kennel has enjoyed a remarkable run of success. Storres Dreadnought and Bonnertyke Bride were Steve's first introduction to Staffords. However, these dogs were never destined to make the big time, and so Anjacks Red Warrior was purchased, closely followed by a bitch, Jackstaff Heaven Sent, from Jack and Marie Kinsley. This bitch swiftly won her Junior Warrant, and was then mated to Ch. Teutonic Warrior. Two pups resulted, Jackstaff Kubla Khan and Jackstaff Prima Donna. Heaven Sent returned to the show ring to win her title, and was mated on three subsequent occasions. Her third litter was sired by her grandson, Jackstaff Rustic Prince, and produced the Champions, Jackstaff Forget-Me-Not and Jackstaff Fatal Attraction.

It was Jackstaff Prima Donna who proved to be the big winner in the show ring. She was awarded a total of five CCs, and is the only Staffordshire Bull Terrier bitch to date to win a Terrier Group. On this occasion she beat the West Highland White Terrier, Ch. Olac Moon Pilot, the dog who went on to win Best in Show at Crufts. Ch. Jackstaff Prima Donna was mated to Boldmore Black Sabbath, and one of the two resulting puppies was Jackstaff Rustic Prince, who went on to sire four Champions.

1990 was a great year for the Jackstaff kennel. Jackstaff Rustic Prince was awarded Top Stud Dog, Ch. Jackstaff Heaven Sent was Top Brood Bitch, and Steve was Top Breeder. Jackstaff Forget-Me-Not, Jackstaff Fatal Attraction and Jackstaff Special Envoy all gained their titles between 1990 and 1991. Ch. Jackstaff Special Envoy (Jackstaff Rustic Prince – Ch. Parkstaff Witch of the North) quickly gained her title, and won a total of fifteen first prizes in the 12-18 months class. When mated to S.A. Ch. Walpark Whiskey Mac at Dumbriton she produced Jackstaff Wise Guy, who is Stud Book qualified and was Best Puppy at Crufts in 1992. Her second

Ch. Jackstaff Heaven Sent: Top Brood Bitch, 1990.

litter, sired by Ch. Ensbury's Little Lad at Shirestaff, produced Jackstaff Johnny Handsome.

Tragically, Ch. Jackstaff Heaven Sent and Ch. Parkstaff Special Envoy died at comparatively young ages, and this has left a large gap in the Jackstaff kennel. However, Steve's skill as a breeder is certain to mean that more stars will soon be on their way.

DUMBRITON

This is my kennel prefix, and I have been fortunate to enjoy considerable success during my time in the breed. My first Stafford bitch was Torosay Black Fern, who gained her title, and one of her offspring went on to sire three British Champions. Following a spell working for a big kennel in the USA, I was asked to buy a couple of puppies for an American breeder. However, the new owner decided the pups should stay in the UK to be campaigned by Danny. One of these puppies, Ch. Pitmax Pasidion of Dumbriton, was to take the show world by storm. He won his title in just ten days – a record that still stands to this day. He went on to win a total of ten CCs and seven Reserve CCs, and is rated by many as the greatest red dog of all time.

There was another star waiting in the wings, and when Skerry Dhu of Dumbriton made his debut at Crufts (having been shown on only one previous occasion), he won Best Puppy, and from that moment he was unbeatable, winning twenty-six classes in succession and gaining his title on the way. The current top dog at Dumbriton is Ch. Debrella Taboo Dhu of Dumbriton, Top Stafford in the UK in 1993.

RECENT SUCCESSES
The Staffordshire Bull Terrier is currently one of the most popular of the Terrier breeds in the UK with recent registrations totalling 5,000 a year. However, this has always been a breed where kennels keep a few dogs who are also family companions. There is not a tradition, as in other breeds, where large kennels keep big numbers of dogs, and produce impressive lists of Champions. Looking at the numbers of Champions who have gained their titles over last few years, it is clear that they come from almost as many individual breeders.

Ch. Torosay Black Fern: My first Champion Stafford.

Ch. Pitmax Pasidion of Dumbrition: This dog took the show world by storm, winning his title in just ten days.

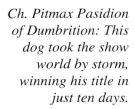

Ch. Debrella Taboo Dhu at Dumbriton: Top Stafford in 1993.

Raymond.

CHAMPIONS: 1990
BITCHES
Ch. Waystaff Bold as Brass
Ch. Tenax Christmas Star
Ch. Makeready Huntsmans Lass
Ch. Kalahari Queen
Ch. Jacsktaff Forget-Me-Not

DOGS
Ch. Bonzaries Kelly Boy
Ch. Chewbacca the Wookie
Ch. Eastaff Lil Stotter
Ch. Langrove Malster
Ch. Rogue Saga

1991
BITCHES
Ch. Alidav the Bedford Squatter
Ch. Bated Breath at Constones
Ch. Fromestaff Nettle at Wyrefare
Ch. Indianna Jet Setter
Ch. Jackstaff Fatal Attraction
Ch. Judael Magic Noire
Ch. Mintmar Mean Marlene
Ch. Mistress McGrath of Boldmore
Ch. Parkstaff Special Envoy at Jackstaff
Ch. Tikkurilan Giddy Kipper

DOGS
Ch. Takiron Dark Destroyer
Ch. Tofo O' Henry
Ch. Lethal Weapon of Crashkon
Ch. Ebony Dreadnought
Ch. Caballero Fire Fighter
Ch. Bullseye of Dogan

Ch. Indiana Jet Setter: Top Puppy, 1990.

Ensbury's Little Lad at Shirestaff: Awarded his title in 1992.

1992
BITCHES
Ch. Zabaretts Razzle Dazzle
Ch. Yorkstaff Silver saga
Ch. White of Morn
Ch. Midnight Huntress
Ch. Clairwell Lady in Red
Ch. Judael Masquerade

DOGS
Ch. Vee's Dream Boy
Ch. Pitbar Rebel Warlord
Ch. Kablice Midnight Caller
Ch. Boldbull Black Jack
Ch. Ensbury's Little Lad at Shirestaff
Ch. Hot Pursuits

Ch. Bourtie Heat Seeker, owned and bred by David and Ann Dick.

Raymond.

1993
BITCHES
Ch. Alpaka Honky Tonk Woman
Ch. Oxtobers Precious Gem
Ch. Debrella Taboo Dhu at Dumbriton
Ch. Bourtie Heat Seeker
Ch. Antrobian Dancing Brave

DOGS
Ch. Sheer Khan
Ch. Ramblix Roberto
Ch. Boldmore Finbar Fury
Ch. Pantycelyn Hagler
Ch. Homestaff King Arthur
Ch. Chrowenda Dark Destroyer.

Gibbs

*Ch. Pantycelyn
Hagler:
Awarded his title
in 1993.*

*Ch. Staffmaster
Pure Opium
(Lancstaff Kjells
Namsos Noble –
Jackstaff Touch
and Go at
Staffmaster):
Top Stafford
bitch, 1994.*

John Hartley.

Crossguns Revolution, owned by Billy Blacker: Top Puppy 1994 and winner of more firsts at Championship Shows than any other puppy in the history of the breed.

1994

BITCHES
Ch. Staffmaster Pure Opium: Top Bitch
Ch. Crashkcon High Society of Broadwar
Ch. Cool As Ice
Ch. Judeal Dark Reality of Cavestaff
Ch. Mary Queen of Staffs at Vulcanstaff
Ch. Stormstaff Sky's The Limit
Ch. Fromstaff Abricadabra of Wyrestaff
Ch. Quarterflash War Squaw

DOGS
Ch. Eaststar Ultimate Warrior
Ch. Yorkstaff Crackerjack
Ch. Domino Flashy Lad: Top Stafford
Ch. Sparstaff Dominator
Ch. Glowood Red Image.

Crossguns Billy Black: An 'outcross' dog with a combination of Dumbriton and Moosskel breeding. These are the two most in-bred lines in the UK.

Ch. Domino Flashy Lad: Top Stafford 1994, winner of the Terrier Group at Bournemouth Championship Show, 1994.

John Hartley.

Swed Ch. Debrella Chianti Dhu of Dumbriton: The only Staffordshire Bull Terrier to win a Terrier Group in Sweden.

SWEDEN

The first Staffordshire Bull Terriers were imported from the UK in the sixties. Sigvard Olsson of the Sunstaffs kennel imported his first Stafford from Finland in 1968. Her name was Aurastaff Lady Amanitha, bred by Steve Stone,, who was largely responsible for introducing the breed to Scandinavia. Then, in 1969 (with the help of Colin Smith), Sigvard Olsson imported the dog Bringary Constellation from England. He was by Ch. Wallstaff Domio and he turned out to be a very successful stud dog for his owner. Both Constellation and Amanitha became International Champions.

Interest in the Staffordshire Bull Terrier has grown from its small beginnings when only half a dozen were registered with the Swedish Kennel Club to a current registration of around sixty. Kennels who are now making their mark in the breed include: Lexweiler (B. Otterbratt), Emerdale (the Ostmann sisters who founded their kennel on Sunstaff bloodlines, Skyotts (D. Eriksson), and E. Hjalmarsson. When Sigvard Olsson died in 1993, his Sunstaff kennel was taken over by his two daughters.

One of the many winning imports from the UK was his Ch. Debrella Chianti Dhu of Dumbriton, who has made breed history by winning a Terrier Group at one of the big Kennel Club shows.

In 1991 a breed club was formed with around 120 members; Sigvard Olsson was elected chairman The first Specialty BOB winner in 1993 was Sunstaffs Joyful Joker (by Ch. Lawbury Showcase of Cradbury). There was an entry of around thirty, and Colin Smith judged. BOS was Sunstaffs Lady Luck out of Ch. Debrella Chianti Dhu of Dumbriton).

Dk. Ch. Club Ch. Copenhagen winner 1991 and 1992 Nethertonion Boy. Bred by Mr and Mrs G. Westwood in the UK and owned by Jytte and Paul Therkelsen in Denmark.   Dalton.

DENMARK
There are only about thirty Staffordshire Bull Terriers in Denmark. Sadly, the development of the breed in this country has stood still as there have been no Stafford breeders, and prospective puppy-buyers have been reluctant to go abroad in order to acquire as dog. Hopefully, this is now changing; the first litter for many years has been bred in Denmark, and there is increasing public interest in the breed. In 1993 a bitch puppy was imported from the UK, and more imports are being planned.

FINLAND

The 25th jubilee of the Staffordshire Bull Terrier Club in Finland was celebrated with a big show that had an entry of 197. Stafford puppies were judged by Claire Lee; Stafford dogs were judged by Jan Hunter, and the bitches were judged by William Hunter. All-American Staffordshire Terriers were judged by Hans van der Berg from Holland.

BOB came from the junior class: his name was Hoppingham's Bullshit (SFCH Kytokarun Star Pride – Hoppingham's Furious Flea). He was bred by Anita Kipelainen, who owns him in partnership with M. and P. Ostamo and J. Tumppila. Best Opposite Sex was Hoppingham Bullshit's half-sister, SFCH Kytokarun Star Pride – Owelan Kismet), who became a Champion on the day. She is owned by her breeders, Irmeli and Matti Sauno in partnership with Kirsti Baston.

Best veteran was SFCH Gallant Quiet Man (Pitmac the Prince of Skelstaff – Just Bonny). He was bred in England by E. Galvin and is owned by Matti Sauno. Best Breeders Class was won by the Hoppingham kennel, owned by Anita Kilpelainen. Best Progeny Class was won by SFCH Kytokarun Star Pride with his offspring. Star Pride is by Ch. Gallant Ringmaster out of Ch. Kytokarun Kissing Girl. He was bred by Anja Virtanen and is owned by S. Tumppila.

Finnish Ch. Gallant Quiet Man, pictured at five years of age.

Finnish Ch. Owelan Mister Mystery: Top Staffordshire Bull Terrier in 1991, Finnish winner 1992.

Dutch, Germ. Int. World Ch. Tenacious Just Kidding.

HOLLAND

The Staffordshire Bull Terrier was first introduced to Holland by Arie van Herpen and Nicolai Grishkov during the late sixties. The first two dogs brought over from the UK were Martyrs Dutch Joe, owned by Nicolai, and Sevenoaks Slenkge, owned by Arie van Herpen. These dogs were mated, and from the resulting two puppies, one became Dutch and International Ch. Melmar's Admiral Avalanche.

Although it was these two breeders who introduced the Stafford to Holland, Nicolai Griskov died in 1979, and so it was Arie van Herpen who is really responsible for establishing the breed in its new home. Another important dog of these early days was Warmaid of Wineva, who gave birth to several Dutch Champions.

The Staffordshire Bull Terrier Club Nederland was established in 1975, starting with a membership of fifty-three. It took a couple of years for the club to grow, and thanks to the ever-increasing popularity of the Stafford, current membership is around 500. Staffords have been imported from a number of countries, and there is a significant increase of litter registrations in Holland.

Melmar's Lady Sarah, bred by Arie van Herpen, owned by Mrs M. Kust-te Kolste.

NORTH AMERICA

After many years of concentrated effort by a band of dedicated Staffordshire Bull Terrier people, the American Kennel Club admitted the breed to the Stud Book in October, 1974. It was not until March, 1975, however, that the breed gained admission to the Terrier Group at AKC shows. Before then, the breed was shown in the Miscellaneous classes.

LEADING DOGS AND KENNELS

A great dog by the name of Gamecock Another Brinsley Lad, owned by Claude Williams of Maryland, was shown by the renowned professional handler, Damara Bolte. Brinsley Lad was the first Staffordshire Bull Terrier to win a Terrier Group in the United States of America.

One of the top dogs in the USA at the time was another great dog called USA Champion Silverzend Satan, born June 18th, 1974. His sire was Ch. Bringarry Dangerman, ex Ch. Constables Billyclub of Silverlake, bred by Jenny and Dana Merritt of Trugrip Kennels. Satan was owned by Jim Davenport, Judi Daniels and Louise Rank. This great dog was the top American-bred Staffordshire Bull Terrier for 1975, 76, 77, and 78. He was also the top Stud dog in the USA for 1979. His wins included 67 Best of Breed, plus 11 Terrier Group placements. The Merritts, Satan's breeders, started their Trugrip kennels in 1969 and are, without any doubt, two of the top American breeders of the present day, having bred some 27 champions.

The young Zane Smith imported UK Champion Reetuns Lord Jim (winner of nine Challenge Certificates) from Albert Wood. This dog was a very striking brindle who was a loss to the United Kingdom, but a great asset to the States. Lord Jim took over from Satan as the new sensation, and lost no time in gaining his title in the USA, which he later followed up by gaining his titles in Mexico and Canada. He was the first Stafford to win a Terrier Group in the USA, at Wallkill, New York, the first of three Group wins that also go into the record books for the 1970s. He was also the first Staffordshire Bull Terrier to win a Group in Mexico. The great Jim was the top winning Stafford in the United States for 1977 and 1978, and was also top Stud dog in 1980. His record at stud was very impressive, with a list of Champions to his credit.

In New Jersey, the Piltdown Kennels of Ed and Stella Rowland have always been a force to reckon with, right from the early days, and thanks are due to them for imports such as American/Canadian Ch. Millgarth Powerpack CD, who produced some top-class progeny. Ed also imported the notable bitch Am.Ch. Red Polly of Salken, who was later owned by Dr & Mrs Jefferies.

Probably the most important American-bred dog to arrive on the Show scene was Am.Ch. Guardstock Red Atom. His sire was Darton of Henstaff and his dam Wystaff Witchcraft, Wystaff being the kennel name of the late Mrs Gwen Galimore. Her kennels also had the distinction of producing the first Stafford to win Best in Show at an all-breeds Championship Show in the United Kingdom, namely Ch. Wystaff Warfare, handled by the teenage Martin Phillips. In the USA, Am.Ch. Guardstock Red Atom made history by being the first Stafford to win Best in Show at an all-breeds Champion Show in America. Thus we had the first Staffords to win Best in Show on both sides of the Atlantic at all-breed Championship shows, both out of Wystaff bitches. Gwen Gallimore would indeed have been very proud.

Red Atom is owned by Judi Daniels and Joe Leblanc, and lives with Judi in California. Atom's first Best in Show was gained at quite a young age, and was a new high for the breed, which had only recently been admitted to the Stud book of the American Kennel Club in 1974. Without doubt, Red Atom has been one of the breed's top show dogs. His win at Mississippi Coast Kennel Club in 1986 brought his total of Terrier Group wins to 26, out of 145 Group placements.

All three of these great dogs have left their mark on the breed by repeatedly siring Champion

Am. Ch. Trugrip Mannstaff Snow Angel. The Trugrip kennel, owned by Jenny and Dana Merritt, is one of the most successful and influential Stafford kennels in the USA.

Am. Ch. Trugrip Lyda Rose A Rair-Find.

offspring. Their invaluable contribution to the breed in America goes without saying. Without Satan, Lord Jim and Red Atom, Staffordshire Bull Terriers would not be held in their current high esteem in the USA.

THE STAFFORDSHIRE BULL TERRIER CLUB

The Staffordshire Bull Terrier Club (incorporated) is doing a great job for the breed in the USA. The people behind this Club are trying their best to educate the layman in the virtues of owning a Stafford, with his tremendous breed characteristics, such as love of children, intelligence, and guarding ability. They also publish Staff Status, a very informative magazine that keeps enthusiasts up-to-date with what is going on in the Stafford world. Mrs Steinman of Michigan City, Indiana, owns two Staffords, the first being the Australian import, Am.Ch. Pumptail Dragonstar Dancer, Utility Dog, Canadian CDX. Dancer had a very easy passage to her title and, when it was time for her to be bred from, the Steinmans used the famous Red Atom. From this mating came the exciting American and Canadian Champion Steinstaff Go In for the Gusto, who was the outstanding puppy in the litter. Mrs Steinman trained both Dancer and Gusto through to their Show and Obedience titles herself. She is owed a debt of gratitude for her hard work in bringing to the public's attention the fact that this great little dog has the ability to win in the Obedience ring as well as the Show ring.

The USA has imported a number of very good dogs from the UK and Australia, dogs like UK and Am. Champion Rellim Task Force, owned by Steve and Denise Eltinge. He was bred in the UK by Jack Miller, and previously owned by Clive and Audrey Hubery, and Am. Ch. Chainmaker's Samsung Of Rikamia.

SOUTH AFRICA
By Gareth Westerdale

The last two decades have seen a meteoric rise in popularity for the Staffordshire Bull Terrier in South Africa. The challenge offered by this preferred position has been enthusiastically accepted by a core of concientious breeders, and their efforts have culminated in our current top-quality, world-class stock. However, we must all guard against the dangers of indiscriminate, commercially orientated breeding – a practice which all true Stafford breeders abhor and are doing their best to end.

THE PIONEERS

The history of the Staffordshire Bull Terrier in South Africa can be most simply classified into the period prior to the formation of the Staffordshire Bull Terrier Club of the Transvaal, and the period after it was founded in 1970. Before the existence of the Club, the Staffordshire Bull Terrier in S.A. was hardly known at all, and entries at shows were very low, to the extent that at most shows outside the Transvaal, there were usually no entries at all.

During this period, the main breeders were Mr and Mrs Frank Walker and Derek Zinn in the Transvaal, and Mrs Glenda Johnston in Cape Town. Mrs Johnston bred many good Staffords at her Dinna Ken kennels. However, since Cape Town is 1,000 miles from Johannesburg, very little of her breeding was seen in the Transvaal. The first Stafford registered with the Kennel Union of South Africa belonged to Mrs C. Draper of Bulawayo. It was imported from the UK in 1947 and registered as Micy's Sprog.

The first S.A. Champion was imported from Scotland. This dog had already won third place in Puppy and Novice classes at the Scottish S.B.T.C. show of 1962, where the judge that day was

S.A. Ch. Magiliam Bronx Bull of Tenacious: The dog that changed the breed in South Africa, imported by Rob Duplooy.

none other than the Joe Mallem of Crossguns fame. The dog, Dungoyne Silent, was imported by Captain G.A. Winter to S.A. in 1962, and went on to win 15 Challenge Certificates. He was the sire of the first S.A.-bred Champion, Ch. Allwin Tawny Tisiphone, who won nine CCs. In 1966 Mr and Mrs R.H. Field of Pietermaritzburg imported two Constones Staffords from Nat Cairns. Constones Cock-A-Hoop and the bitch Constones Colonsia each won two CCs in 1956-7. The dog was sired by UK Ch. Constones Eastaff This'll Do, and the bitch by Constones Cadet.

THE BREED DEVELOPS

By 1967, a total of 100 Staffords had been registered with K.U.S.A. Almost twenty years later, in one year alone (1985), a total of 1,778 Staffords were registered in South Africa. One of the best Staffords ever imported from the UK — S.A. Ch. Mayfairs Bunninyong Julius, bred by Mr and Mrs Wiltshire — was brought to S.A. in 1964 by Mr Joshua of Bloemfontein. Unfortunately, there were very few Staffords in the Bloemfontein area, and this magnificent Stafford was virtually lost to breed. Dr Nagal of Meyerton imported five dogs and bitches from John Gordon, but retired from the Stafford scene many years ago. Many of the pedigrees in the sixties and early seventies had these dogs in them.

One of the first dogs which Frank and Dora Walker introduced to their Frandors Kennels was S.A. Ch. Meyerton Murphy, whom they purchased from Colin Auret. The Walkers imported two Staffords from Ken Fenson to improve their stock. S.A. Ch. Frandors Pitbull Jess made a tremendous impact on the breed in S.A. by siring the record of five S.A. Champions. Unfortunately, the imported dog, Frandors Brian Boru of Cuileog, died at a young age, siring only two litters before his tragic death. One of his granddaughters, S.A. Ch. Pitstaff Felicity, was Best of Breed at the Transvaal Clubs Trophy Show in 1976, under Mr Nat Cairns. Cuileog is the kennel name of Billy Richard of Eire. Derek Zinn also bred and showed one of the stars of the period, S.A. Ch. Fiery Blackie, who was grandsire of S.A. Ch. Caesar of Woburn.

In 1968 Andre Hartzemberg started his Chainmakers kennels and became a force to be reckoned

S.A. Ch. The Brown Bomber of Westmax: KUSA's Top Dog 1989, and the most prolific show winner of all time with a total of fifty-six BOBs at Championship shows. Owned by Gareth Westerdale.

with for the next ten years or so. Andre had three champions in his kennels, namely S.A. Ch. Frandors Doncaster Laddie, S.A. Ch. Frandors Perfect Lady, and an imported bitch, S.A. Ch. Wirswall Oyez It's Me. S.A. Ch. Frandors Doncaster Laddie was the winner of 21 CCs and 21 Best of Breeds.

THE TRANSVAAL CLUB
The Staffordshire Bull Terrier Club of the Transvaal was formed in 1970, with Frank Walker as its first Chairman. After the formation of the club, the popularity of the Stafford increased by leaps

S.A. Ch. Visstaff Invincible Mile of Chassuki, owned by Charles and Suki Woods.

and bounds. The Trophy show in 1975 attracted the most entries ever – 127 dogs and bitches. The judge on this occasion was Jim Bolton from the UK.

The Transvaal Club holds three shows a year, two Open shows and a Championship show. The Club Trophy show is held in conjunction with the famous Goldfields Championship show. Henry Pretorius, the doyen of dog shows in S.A., is the man in charge of Goldfields, and has been a great friend to the breed. In fact, it was Henry who came up with the idea of bringing a Stafford specialist to judge at Goldfields Championship show every year.

Judges and BoB winners:

Year	Judge	Best of Breed
1971	Jean Newby-Frazer (USA)	S.A.Ch. Frandors Doncaster Laddie
1972	Wallie Baron (Rhodesia)	S.A.Ch. Frandors Doncaster Laddie
1973	George Downs (UK)	S.A.Ch. Frandors Doncaster Laddie
1974	Ron Servat (UK)	S.A.Ch. Blackcountry Konker (imp)
1975	Jim Bolton (UK)	S.A.Ch. Blackcountry Konker
1976	Nat Cairns (UK)	S.A.Ch. Pitstaffs Felicity

1977	Alex Waters (UK)	S.A.Ch. Pitstaffs justin
1978	Lionel Hemstock (UK)	S.A.Ch. Danny Boy of Dafto
1979	Ken Fenson (UK)	S.A.Ch. Pitstaffs Justin
1980	Nancy Bolton (UK)	S.A.Ch. Bosheda Devil
1981	John Beikie (SA)	Int.Ch. Pitbull Red Regent (imp)
1982	Les Aspin (UK)	Int.Ch. Pitbull Red Regent (imp)
1983	Ian Ellison (UK)	S.A.Ch. Lintanas Guy
1984	Nat Cairns (UK)	Badliers Reeza
1985	Terry Giles (UK)	S.A.Ch.Magliam The Bronxbull of Tenacious (imp)
1986	George Walton (UK)	S.A.Ch. Tenacious Kojak
1987	Mike Holman (UK)	S.A.Ch. Betchgreen Dark Desire (imp)
1988	Paul Wilkinson (UK)	K.U.S.A. National Ch. The Brown Bomber of Westmax
1989	Vera Westwood (UK)	S.A.Ch. Marconn Dynamic Showman
1990	Judi Daniels (USA)	S.A.Ch. Cravonpark Billy
1991	Barbara Fournier (USA)	S.A.Ch. Pitwar The Great Pretender
1992	Bryn Cadogan (UK)	S.A.Ch. Sandi of Pitwar
1993	George Walton (UK)	C h. (Zim.) Goldboy of Gamestaff

All these judges are treated to a visit to the prestigious Kruger Game Reserve for a week, and a memorable stay in South Africa, visiting many Stafford folk in their homes. The importance of having an unbiased specialist was once again proved in the selection of Terry Giles, who judged in 1985. An entry of 107 awaited him. Gilsie is a fearless judge and very professional in his approach to his job, in which he has been a great ambassador for the UK during his many visits abroad.

THE PRETORIA STAFFORDSHIRE BULL TERRIER CLUB
ESTABLISHED 1982

Activities: Annual Championship show held during June and which has broken the record for the largest entry at a breed show in SA for three years with 203 exhibits in 1989, 228 in 1991 and 257 in 1992. Club policy is to invite a UK specialist judge to officiate, the club then hosts a breed clinic presented by the visiting judge. The club holds open shows every February and September as well as handling classes prior to their shows. Their calendar also features an annual prizegiving with winners parade, as well as a dinner/dance.

Publications: PSBTC produce a quarterly newsletter. The annual yearbook entitled "The Ring" has expanded to the point where the 1991/2 edition boasted a full colour glossy cover together with 160 pages, and was acknowledged by many as the best ever breed club publication in South Africa.

Current Executive Committee: Chairman: Gareth Westerdale. Vice Chairman: Petrus Retief. Treasurer: Gerhard Oosthuizen. Secretary: Juanita Hobbs.

Address: P O Box 4321, Pretoria, 0001.

Current Membership: Approximately 340.

Comments: At this point in time, the largest and most active Stafford Club in South Africa.

S.A. Ch. Pitwar The Great Pretender: Best in Show Goldfields, 1991.

S.A. Ch. Jodel's Upton Girl: Winner of some twenty-three CCs and the only bitch to qualify for Junior Dogmore Dog of the Year and Dogmore Dog of the Year in the same year – 1992.

Ch.(Zim.)
Goldenboy of
Gamestaff:
Stafford of the Year
in Zimbabwe 1992,
1993, 1994, Terrier
of the Year 1992,
Stud Dog of the
Year 1993.

INFLUENTIAL IMPORTS

Since the formation of the Transvaal Club, a number of UK-bred Staffords have been imported to South Africa, thereby raising the standard of the breed considerably. Between 1971 and 1973, three Staffords were imported by the Pitstaffs kennels. All three became S.A. champions. S.A. Blackcountry Konker was bred by Betty Deuce and arrived in S.A. in 1971. Sired by UK Ch. Rapparee Rothersyke Vow ex Linksbury Gertrude, Konker won BoB at the Trophy show twice, and was BIS at the Rhodesian Stafford Club's Trophy show in 1975. He sired many BoB and CC winners. S.A. Ch. Catrin of Linksbury produced very sound Staffords. A characteristic worth noting is that not one of her three litters had bad dentition. Her first litter produced S.A.Ch. Pitstaffs Ferdinand of Brookdale and S.A.Ch. Pitstaffs Felicity of Tenacious, although there were only three puppies in the litter. The third imported Stafford, S.A.Ch. Pitstaffs Golden Cracker of Linksbury, won his Champion title at 11 months, winning four CCs and one Reserve CC in his first five Championship shows. Cracker's most notable son was S.A.Ch. Pitstaff Justin, who won BoB twice at the Trophy show.

Derek Zinn's S.A.Ch. Hartfels Ashstock Pearl Buttons, bred by Alex Waters, won CCs at the Trophy shows and in Rhodesia. Her son, S.A.Ch. Armunks Georgie of Linkcroft, sired by Blackcountry Konker, became a Champion in 1976. In 1971 Bob Train brought a lovely red bitch, Kingstaff Leo Girl, with him to S.A. She was by Dennybeck Hard Diamond and Ashstock Valkyroe, and soon became a S.A.Ch. Her litter by S.A. Ch. Blackcountry Konker produced S.A. Ch. Hammers Harlequin Bess. Mated to Chainmakers Gazo Grande of Boshada, she produced S.A. Ch. Hammers Laddie of Quintessence.

Another S.A. import of the seventies who made her mark on the breed was Des and Dawn Brown's S.A. Ch. Stayfield Black Bess, producer of another Trophy winner in S.A. Ch. Boshada Devil. S.A. Ch. Chainmakers Gazo-Grande of Boshada, bred by Andre Hartzemberg and owned by Des Brown, was a prolific winner, collecting CCs and BoBs at most of the Championship shows from Cape Town to Johannesburg. 'Rip' also won a CC at the Trophy show in 1976, and was Stafford of the Year twice. As a stud dog, he produced eight S.A. Champions.

In 1978 Rob and Eleanor Duplooy added Venlas Pied Piper of Tenacious to their kennel. 'Barney', as he was known, sired three S.A. Champions from three different bitches, namely S.A. Ch. Hammers Barrow Boy, S.A. Ch. Tenacious Contessa and S.A. Ch. Brookdales Viscount.

One of the most important imports so far is S.A. Ch. Magliam The Bronxbull of Tenacious, full litter brother of UK Ch. Redstaff King and UK Ch. The Malaser Mauler. These three brothers were all bred by Billy Pearson (Magliam) UK. The Bronxbull was four and a half years old when Danny Gilmour discovered him in the back streets of Liverpool when he was looking for a red dog for Rob Duplooy.

Chapter Fifteen

HEALTH CARE

DIAGNOSIS AND TREATMENT

If a human appears to be ill or out of sorts, it is usually comparatively easy to find out what is wrong. The patient can describe the discomfort and pinpoint where it is located. A canine patient is very much at a disadvantage as there can be no verbal communication of symptoms – although much can be learnt by observing behaviour. It was thought that most dogs had a higher pain threshold than humans, but modern veterinary thinking suggests that animals feel the same level of pain as human beings, but are unable to express it as we can. Consequently, greater emphasis is now being put on the use of analgesics (painkillers) in the veterinary world, in situations where their use would be routine for humans. It is now a matter of attempting to determine the seriousness of the condition by way of observation, although, as with humans, reaction to pain varies greatly between individual dogs.

PREVENTATIVE MEASURES

Prevention is, of course, far better than cure, and by following a few simple and basic rules a good deal of discomfort and illness can be avoided. The first, and one of the most important measures, is the provision of a regular diet of fresh and nourishing food. Both humans and canines are better able to resist disease and infection if fed a good diet. Just as vital to your dog's health is the provision of clean, dry living quarters, with well-aired clean bedding. There must always be a plentiful supply of fresh drinking water which should be changed frequently.

Staffordshire Bull Terriers are generally a healthy breed. They do not have the 'exaggerations' of some of the fancy breeds, and so they do not suffer from some of the conditions that affect other breeds. The most important rule is to keep a close watch on your dog so that you can detect any unexpected change in appearance or behaviour at the earliest possible stage. If you suspect that something is amiss, you must then determine the seriousness of the condition and decide whether professional advice should be sought. If there is any doubt at all in your mind, give your veterinary surgeon a ring and be on the safe side.

SYMPTOMS OF ILL HEALTH

There are a number of indications that can be warnings of future. These include:

Coughing
Loss of appetite, extending for more than forty-eight hours
Diarrhoea – particularly if there is evidence of blood in the stools
Vomiting

Constipation
Rubbing of the ears, eyes or mouth
Anal pain, manifested by rubbing affected area
Scratching
Sleeping more than usual
Loss of weight, even though the dog is still eating well
Lethargy, with the dog showing no interest in normal activities and pastimes
Limping and favouring one leg
Pain when touched
Obvious pain when walking, can indicate one or more of a number of ailments
Tiredness following exercise (i.e. reduced exercise tolerance)
Excessive thirst (bearing in mind that a dog will drink a lot more in hot weather, and a nursing bitch will need a greater fluid intake than normal).

PARASITES
The term parasite may be defined as an animal or plant living in or upon another, and drawing nutrients directly from it. There are many parasites that can live off your dog, if proper care and precautions have been neglected. Parasites can be divided into internal (endoparasites) and external (ectoparasites), and the treatment differs for the two types.

ENDOPARASITES
In the main, internal parasites comprise of worms of various kinds, and it is essential to adopt a strict worming programme in order to keep your dog free of these parasites. The commonest type of endoparasites to be encountered are:

HOOKWORM (Uncinaraia Stendcephaia): This is the northern or cold climate hookworm. The small, round worms of 3/4 of an inch (2cms) in length live in the small intestine. Transmission of this hookworm is facilitated when a number of dogs use the same grass exercising runs, or if you feed sheep's intestine raw.

WHIPWORM (Trichuris Vulpis): This also occurs in larger kennels where numbers of dogs use the same grass area. The whipworm grows to 3ins (7cms) in length, and is found in the caecum.

LUNGWORM (Filaroides Osleri): This is found in nodules in the trachea and brochii. It is the third parasite often found in larger kennels, and it often poses some difficulties in diagnosis and treatment. Some cases are symptomless, but others cause a dry, racking cough.

TAPEWORM (Dipylidium Caninum): This infests the small intestine of dogs. It grows up to 20ins (50cms) in length, and its life cycle includes fleas and many other animals as intermediate hosts.

ROUNDWORM (Toxicara Canis): Control of this parasite is of the greatest importance because humans, especially children, are particularly at risk. The worm measures up to 6ins (15cms) in length, and, as the name suggests, it is round and white. The minute eggs can be ingested by children or by other dogs from the ground, from the fur, or from bedding. It is essential that you clear up after your dog immediately.

HEARTWORM: This parasite is not often seen in the United Kingdom or Europe, but it is endemic in tropical and subtropical areas of Asia, Australia, Central America, and parts of the USA where mosquitoes transmit the larval form of the worm. Treatment is by means of a daily (prophylactic) tablet, but it is reported that the introduction of a new drug has reduced the worming programme to one tablet each month. If an imported dog is found to be infested, successful treatment can sometimes be carried out in two or three days.

To prevent endoparasitic infestation, I can only re-emphasise the importance of adopting a regular worming programme, which must be strictly adhered to throughout the lifetime of the dog. If you are uncertain about the type of worm your dog may be carrying, you will need to obtain a sample of faeces and take it to your vet, who will be able to identify the parasite and advise on the appropriate treatment.

ECTOPARASITES
Ectoparasites are parasites living outside the body, on the body, or in the skin. The most frequent and easy discernible sign is pruritus or persistent, severe itching. Scratching temporarily relieves the itching by substituting overriding pain sensations, but skin damage can result. It is therefore most important to treat the cause of the trouble. The main ectoparasites that affect canines are listed below:

MANGE
SARCOPTIC MANGE (Scabies): This is caused by the parasitic mite Sarcoptes Scabei Canis. It burrows into the epidermis and the female lays her eggs there. Itching is intense, but this does not develop until some time after infestation is established, and so the signs could be taken as those of some other condition. This condition is almost impossible to treat successfully unless you catch it as near to the beginning of the cycle as possible. I recommend treating with Benzyl Benzoate. This is an old-fashioned remedy but, in my experience, it is most effective. It needs to be rubbed on to the affected area, being careful to avoid the eyes. The symptoms are considerable irritation of head, ears and elbows. The mites can be killed if precautions are taken, but re-infestation is always possible.
DEMODECTIC MANGE: This is caused by a different mite, and although it does not cause as much irritation, it is very difficult to get rid of. Again, I have found that Benzyl Benzoate is the most effective cure. Demodectic mange usually starts with a single bare patch which looks dirty-grey in colour.

FLEAS: Fleas cause pruritus by simple mechanical irritation – crawling on the skin – but bites can also be irritating. Clinically, flea allergy dermatitis is also known as summer eczema, and it is accompanied by severe itching and an exudative dermititus, which can be aggravated by the efforts of the dog to relieve the condition. Treatment and prevention of flea infestations can be long and drawn out – cats sometimes provide a ready supply of fleas for re-infestation, and so they must also receive attention. Once a dog has become infested, flea collars and medication are rarely enough without other treatment.

An effective method of combating flea infestation is to bath the dog every week or so for about a month. The bath should contain an insecticidal agent that will kill the fleas. The dead fleas can then be groomed out with a fine-toothed comb. It is essential that *all* bedding places where the dog has been are thoroughly treated to prevent any recurrence.

LICE: This can also be a problem, particularly in groups of puppies (in breeding kennels or pet shops). Infestation is usually around the head and neck and causes severe itching. Bathing in insecticidal shampoo is usually effective.

TICKS: These can be picked up in areas where sheep graze. Do not try to pull them off, as you will probably leave the head intact under the skin. The most effective treatment is to apply some alcohol spirit which will result in the tick dropping off.

HARVEST MITES: These mites can be found in straw, hay, grain and carpets, and occur most frequently in the summer and autumn. The straw mite occupies hay, grain and straw, and it causes itching in both dogs and humans. Generally, veterinary advice should be sought if the cause is not obvious and the cure not sure and simple.

EAR MITES: Ear mites cannot be seen by the naked eye, but they cause severe irritation in the ear. Immediate treatment is needed as they can very easily be transmitted from one animal to another.

INFECTIOUS DISEASES

There are a number of conditions where prophylactic inoculation is necessary to control the infection and prevent the onset of the disease. It is essential that this programme of inoculation is discussed with your veterinary advisor at an early stage.

CANINE DISTEMPER

This is can be found in young, unvaccinated dogs of any breed. The peak period for infection is between three and six months. Onset of the condition can happen rapidly; it is often proceeded by coughing, vomiting, diarrhoea and signs of fever. However, if a dog has been regularly vaccinated, it is very unlikely to get distemper. There is no specific cure for the disease. Broad spectrum antibiotics help to control secondary infection, but they have no effect on the virus itself.

As the condition is generally to be found in very young dogs, it is essential that the puppy is vaccinated at an early age. The presence of maternal antibodies controls the condition until the puppy may be safely vaccinated without fear of neutralisation. One of the signs of canine distemper is a thickening of the pads, which gave it the name "hardpad", but this is not a commonly seen symptom. If you suspect your dog has distemper, ask your vet to come to your home, rather than taking a potentially infectious dog to the surgery.

LEPTOSPIROSIS

Leptospirosis comes in two forms, one of which generally affects the kidneys, and the other, the liver. There may be an overlap and one bacterium has an association with the other condition. Preventative inoculation has drastically reduced the incidence of infection by these bacteria.
LEPTOSPIRA CANICOLA: This occurs mainly in urban areas and affects the kidneys. Luckily, most dogs suffer only a relatively mild infection. If the condition is severe, it can result in kidney failure. Both strains of Leptospirosis can affect man. Administration of antibiotics by your veterinary surgeon can clear up the infection. Prevention is better than cure.
LEPTOSPINA ICTEROHAEMORRHAGIAE: This is a bacterium carried by rats, and the disease can be transferred to dogs and also to humans, when it is called Weils disease. It is thus important to exercise care if contact is made with an infected dog. The dog will pass the bacteria in urine during the infection, and for months afterwards. Disinfection is not easy, and inoculation is the answer.

CANINE PARVOVIRUS

The method of infection is generally by mouth, and because the virus is very resistant to destruction, large amounts of infected faeces are deposited into the environment. The condition can affect a dog at any age, but it is most frequent in puppies. The signs that are most common in dogs are severe vomiting, followed by diarrhoea, weight loss and dehydration. If the dog is to survive, fluid replacement therapy is essential, as well as a thorough disinfecting of the premises.

Parvovirus is resistant to most disinfectants. Formaldehyde and bleach are effective for a short time only, as they are made non-effective by organic material. There are, however, very effective parvocidal disinfectants available. Ask your vet for advice.

PARAINFLUENZA (Kennel Cough)

This condition is caused by a virus. Bordatella is the organism that probably causes most outbreaks of kennel cough. Droplet infection is contracted by inhaling infected air, and it is generally transmitted from one dog to another.

The most obvious sign of infection is a sharp cough. Adult dogs may continue to eat and behave normally, but the situation can be more serious in puppies and in older dogs. A vaccine, which is pushed up the nasal passages by a syringe, forms the basis of preventive treatment. It is probably wise to have a prophylactic inoculation before putting your Staffordshire Bull Terrier into a boarding kennels, as kennel cough is highly infectious.

INFECTIOUS CANINE HEPATITIS

This is caused by a virus which can be excreted from an infected animal in saliva, faeces or urine – thus all these are possible sources of infection. The virus can be excreted in the urine for more than six months after the dog's recovery. It seems that dog-to-dog contact, or contact with infected material, are the causes of infection spreading. Measures to isolate puppies reduce the likelihood of the disease. Puppies in their first year are the most susceptible. Signs include loss of appetite, vomiting and diarrhoea, and a jaundice may be seen in the eyes. Some dogs (twenty per cent) that recover from the disease show a corneal oedema (blue eye).

RABIES

This is a fatal condition caused by a virus which attacks the central nervous system. There are various signs of the disease in dogs, but basically it can be divided into 'dumb' or 'furious' rabies. To a large extent, these descriptions are self-explanatory. Furious rabies is comparatively easy to spot – a normally placid dog becomes ferocious. Dumb rabies is harder to detect – the dog is affected by a nerve paralysis, and a normally aloof dog becomes dependant and affectionate. This, though harder to diagnose, is the more common form.

The disease is endemic in many countries – Antarctica and Australia are the only continents free of the condition – although in Europe some countries, including Britain and Ireland, are still not affected by the disease. In Continental Europe the disease is endemic, and it is only the enforcement of strict quarantine laws that has prevented large scale infection in the UK. Following infection by a bite, the saliva of the affected dog carries the virus. The dog seldom lives more than five days from the clinical onset of the disease. Once the brain is infected, it proceeds down the cranial nerves. There is no known cure.

TREATING COMMON AILMENTS

ANAL GLANDS

Sometimes the anal glands, which are just under the skin and slightly below and on each side of the anus, become blocked or impacted and need to be emptied. The most obvious sign that they are not emptying naturally is if the dog drags its bottom along the ground. The vet will empty the glands, but once shown you should be able to do it yourself. The fluid is rather smelly – it is normally excreted when the dog passes a motion to mark his territory.

BITES AND STINGS

Dogs are inquisitive creatures, and it is not unusual for a dog to get stung by a wasp or a bee. If your Stafford is stung by a bee, it will experience considerable pain. Try to locate the sting and pull it out. Wasps do not leave their stings behind, but the area of the sting, or where the bee sting was removed, should be bathed with bicarbonate of soda. If the sting is in the mouth, the area should be swabbed frequently with surgical spirit.

If your dog is bitten by a snake, veterinary attention should be sought straight away. In the meantime, do not allow the dog to move, and try to bandage above the bite. If your dog has a fight and is bitten, keep the wound clean. Do not allow it to heal too quickly or an abscess may form.

CONSTIPATION

This could be the result of a number of causes, but the underlying problem is usually dietary, e.g. too much protein and insufficient roughage. The best prophylactic treatment is correct feeding, providing clean water at all times, and clean, dry bedding in the sleeping quarters. A good, nutritional diet is of the greatest importance in maintaining the health of your dog.

CYSTS (INTERDIGITAL)

These occur between the toes and can be a very painful, usually causing severe lameness. Soaking the affected foot in warm, salt water helps, but the cyst may need lancing. Ask your vet for advice.

EARS

As a breed, Staffordshire Bull Terriers are not prone to ear problems, but unless precautions are taken you could get trouble! Just lift the dog's ear, and look inside to check for red inflammation within the main part of the ear. It is very important not to probe inside the ear. If you see any signs of inflammation, contact your vet for advice.

EYES

Most conditions of the eye require expert help, but bland eye lotions can be used safely when the eyes are inflamed and watering.

HEAT STROKE

This condition is often the result of a careless owner failing to provide sufficient ventilation for dogs left in cars. Should this happen, treatment must be quick in order to be effective. The body temperature has to be lowered by ice-pads or sponges of cold water – ten minutes should be enough to bring the temperature down. If recovery is not fast, seek veterinary attention.

SHOCK

Dogs can easily suffer from shock as the result of a road accident, or because of burns or scalds. Fright and severe pain can also cause shock. The treatment is to keep the dog warm with blankets and with hot-water bottles, if necessary.

SKIN CONDITIONS

Most terriers are prone to skin conditions, and one of the commonest causes is incorrect diet. If your dog has skin problems, check the balance of the diet to ensure there is a correct balance of nutrients. It is also important to check your dog's coat each day. One flea bite can cause the most severe itching, which your dog will try to relieve by scratching. In no time, the dog will have scratched a bare patch, often breaking the skin. This often occurs near the tail or on the hip. Obviously, the source of irritation must be treated, but when it comes to treating bald patches, I have found that a few drops of Evening Primrose Oil, administered daily on the food, will work wonders in getting the hair back.

DANDRUFF: This is another condition that may affect your Stafford but, again, the old faithful lotion, Benzyl Benzoate, is the most effective remedy.

ECZEMA: This occurs in two forms – wet or dry. It is a fairly common skin condition, and treatment consists of applying Benzyl Benzoate on the affected area.

TEETH

A close check should be kept on the mouth in order to ensure that nothing wedges between the teeth. These should be kept clean and devoid of tartar. Dogs love marrow bones which not only keep them amused for hours, but also provide essential nutrition. As a bonus they keep the teeth clean and tartar free. However, do not leave two Staffords alone with a bone – in fact, a dog that is given a bone should always be supervised.

TRAVEL SICKNESS

In order to prevent travel sickness, your dog should be taken for short journey at first, and then gradually build up the distance. If your dog is prone to travel sickness then it is advisable not to feed large meals just before a journey.

VOMITING AND DIARRHOEA

If your dog only vomits on one occasion, this is probably nature's way of getting rid of something that should not have been ingested in the first place, or because the stomach is temporarily out of order. The best treatment is to leave well alone. However, if the vomiting continues, and is accompanied by diarrhoea, all food should be withheld and the dog kept warm. If the dog is weak, and you have also seen evidence of blood in the stools, you should contact your vet immediately.

If there is no blood in the stools, the diarrhoea can often be cured by a change of diet. Withhold food for a period of twenty-four hours (ensuring that fresh water is available), and then offer cooked fish or chicken, with rice instead of biscuit. Call the vet if the condition does not improve.

Breeders' Directory

North East

ADREEAM
Mr R. & Mrs J. Potts,
28 Arbroath Road, Sunderland, Tyne and
Wear SR3 3LB
Tel: 091 565 3787
Dogs at stud. Puppies occasionally for sale.

BRYSTAFF
B. Owen and F. Turner
17 Cambridge Street, South Elmsall, West
Yorkshire WF9 2AW
Tel: 0977 645619
Dogs at stud. Puppies occasionally for sale.

North West

FRITANE
Rita & Fred Adams
Earl Hall, Keighley Road, Laneshawbridge,
Colne,
Lancs. BB8 7EJ.
Tel: 0282 867968
Dogs at stud. Puppies occasionally for sale.
Boarding facilities available.

West Midlands

NETHERTONION
Mr & Mrs G. Westwood
155 Park Road, Netherton, Dudley, West
Midlands DY2 9DD
Tel: 0384 259987
Dogs at stud. Puppies occasionally for sale.